THE
MINDFUL
GUIDE TO
CONFLICT
RESOLUTION

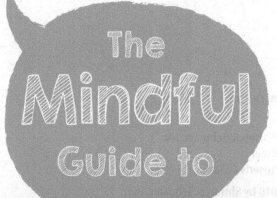

The Mindful Guide to Conflict Resolution

How to Thoughtfully Handle Difficult Situations, Conversations, and Personalities

ROSALIE PUIMAN

Adams Media

New York London Toronto Sydney New Delhi

Adams Media
An Imprint of Simon & Schuster, Inc.
57 Littlefield Street
Avon, Massachusetts 02322

First Adams Media trade paperback edition November 2019

Interior design by Julia Jacintho

10 9 8 7 6 5 4 3 2 1

Library of Congress Cataloging-in-Publication Data has been applied for.

ISBN 978-1-5072-1132-8
ISBN 978-1-5072-1133-5 (ebook)

DEDICATION

To Eiso, who always sees the best in me,
even in our most difficult conversations.

CONTENTS

PART 3: HOW TO APPLY PAUSE IN REAL LIFE 157

ACKNOWLEDGMENTS

To Julia Jacques of Adams Media I am profoundly grateful for trusting me, my writing, and my thoughts on mindful conflict resolution. You saw the author in me. Thank you for bringing this dream into reality.

To my editor Laura Daly I offer my deep gratitude and admiration. Without you it would have been so much harder to make this book what it now is. Thank you for making this such a smooth process and for your words of encouragement and support. A big thanks also to everyone else on the awesome Adams Media team for their talent and creativity, and their hard work behind the scenes.

I am grateful to the many teachers and mentors who supported the conception of the ideas in this book, both in real life and through their books and videos. I specifically want to mention Alan Seale, who introduced me to the power of transformational presence in such a profound way.

To my private clients I want to express deep gratitude for their trust in me. Thank you for helping me bring mindful conflict resolution into form. Your openness and your willingness to learn and explore have been an immense inspiration to me.

I want to thank Martin Dooms, founder of Intermin, the organization that gave me my first job as a young government manager, for his belief in me. I had one of my first really difficult work conversations with you, and your utter acceptance of my side of the story and your appreciation for me speaking my truth have encouraged me to start showing more of myself at work.

I want to thank Kim Taylor, Astrid van Dijk, Maaike Pieters, Cristel Loeb, Aryeh Loeb, Sander Verhoeckx, and Eveline van der Burgh for seeing and loving me in my truth and for cheering me on, every step I take in the direction of my highest potential. I am blessed to have people like you surrounding me.

To Safka Overweel, who has been my friend since we were five years old and who lived through everything with me, I want to say thank you, love, for all the years your friendship has supported me. Nothing I wrote in the chapter on friendships comes from our relationship, as we don't seem to need difficult conversation to constantly deepen our friendship. Thank you for being my friend always.

To my family, both those who are still with me and those who have crossed over, I am deeply grateful for your support and love. Thank you for being in my corner always. And for your impeccable taste in musical guilty pleasures.

To my sister, Liselot Puiman, who is also one of my best friends: I am so grateful for having you in my life. It is beautiful to be able to walk this path with you, to know that you always understand where I come from and where I'm going. Your strength, talent, and deep love are an inspiration to me. I love you, babe!

I am deeply, deeply grateful to my mother, Lilian Withagen. Thank you, Mama, for always lifting me up: for carrying me whenever I needed carrying, for believing in me, for seeing me, for raising me, for loving me. Also, thank you for always being practical and for offering concrete help whenever you feel I need it—the most recent example being this book, which so greatly benefited from your hours of meticulous dedication. I love you so much!

To Eiso Vaandrager, my husband, my beloved: Thank you, my love, for your unwavering support throughout the process of writing this book—for holding me, for cheering me on, and for making me laugh. Also, I am so grateful for your rock-solid presence next to me through all the years of intense empirical research into difficult conversations, speaking my truth, and growing into myself. Thank you for exploring with me what it means to interconnect. You taught me that being able to have an honest, openhearted disagreement means you are loved more, not less. I see you, and I love you so.

To my daughter, Bodil, and my son, Armin: Darlings, thank you for choosing me to be your mama. Thank you for your candor and for allowing me to learn so much. Thank you for always being your true selves. I love you both to the moon and back.

Finally, I thank you, the reader of this book. Thank you for deciding that it is time to change the way you disagree with people. I hope *The Mindful Guide to Conflict Resolution* will support you in expressing everything that needs to be said, while building a stronger connection to yourself and the other person.

INTRODUCTION

Difficult conversations are an unavoidable part of everyday life. Whether it's your colleague failing to deliver her part of your joint project, your father stopping by unannounced after he'd agreed not to, or you and your partner having a disagreement, conflicts big and small can arise in any part of your life.

If you're like most people, these conflicts led to feelings of dread, sadness, annoyance, or fear. You might have tried to avoid facing the problem altogether or dug in your heels and refused to compromise. Maybe after the fight you felt regret, or hoped that in a future argument, things might become easier or better—but the same pattern just repeats itself.

What if you could approach difficult situations in a more thoughtful, kinder, and more constructive way?

What if you could go from reacting (thanks to old experiences and lingering pain) to responding to what is in front of you right now?

What if you could let go of anger, regret, disappointment, resentment, and fear and instead focus on creating a deeper connection with the other party?

What if you could move past worrying about who's winning or losing to finding solutions that both sides can appreciate and support?

You can do all of these things and more with mindful conflict resolution. In mindful conflict resolution, you pay attention to only the present moment, with an attitude of curiosity, openness, and acceptance. You change the endgame from the pointless "winner versus loser" mentality to one where both parties can be right at the same time. The techniques in this book will empower you to build such a strong connection to yourself that you forgo angry and painful reactions and opt for mindful responses instead.

If, for example, you are used to reacting very emotionally to negative feedback, and finding yourself in a heated exchange of accusations as a result, you'll see how applying mindful attitudes like self-trust, acceptance, and interconnection will lead to a completely different experience. Or, if you usually put all your energy into forcing things to happen in a certain way, you will now see how a mindful attitude allows synchronicities and fresh perspectives to come to the forefront.

Every chapter in this book offers you a way to practice these methods so that engaging in tough conversations becomes easier and easier. You will also begin to see the potential that exists in each of these interactions. After all, having the courage to engage in a difficult conversation is a truly powerful opportunity to take your life into your own hands—to grow, to learn, to understand, to connect, to love, and to let go.

The Mindful Guide to Conflict Resolution will inspire you to finally clear up anything and everything you have been swallowing, holding in, and grinding over, while at the same time deepening and strengthening your relationships. Let mindfulness lead the way to a happier, calmer life—one conversation at a time.

PART 1

IDENTIFYING

This first part of *The Mindful Guide to Conflict Resolution* sets the stage for you to think about conflicts in a completely different way. You'll learn what causes difficult conversations in the first place, and why you should actually want to engage in them. You will also see how mindfully approaching difficult conversations leads to an easier and more positive way through them.

During difficult communications, people often focus either on themselves or on the other person, focusing on their own position or on how the other person is doing. Neither of those approaches is ultimately successful. In Chapter 2, you will discover how connecting to both yourself and the other party is the key to successful resolutions.

Chapter 3 dives into the real reasons that difficult conversations are so difficult. People often think that conflicts arise because people disagree about the facts or the best way forward—but that's not really the case. It's actually the highly overlooked issues behind the scenes that often contribute to emotionally charged discussions. You'll learn how to spot that situation and what to do about it.

Let's jump into the important potential behind difficult conversations so you can stop dreading them and start seeing the good that can come out of them.

CHAPTER I

WHAT IS MINDFUL CONFLICT RESOLUTION?

> "Peace is not absence of conflict, but the ability to cope with conflict by peaceful means."
>
> *Ronald Reagan*

This chapter focuses on what it means to bring a mindful approach to handling hard conversations and conflicts. These difficult conversations are the ones that scare you, the ones that challenge you, the ones you try to avoid, the ones you practice in your mind beforehand, and the ones you replay over and over afterward in your head. Learning mindfulness techniques will make those conversations more productive and constructive and leave you feeling satisfied and content instead of drained and disappointed. Let's start transforming how you approach difficult conversations, whether they're with coworkers, family, friends, or romantic partners.

What It Means to Be Mindful in Difficult Situations

Mindfulness is a way of living in the present moment that is based on ancient Buddhist teachings that Jon Kabat-Zinn helped introduce to Western culture in the 1990s. Nowadays, millions of people use mindfulness as a way of life to decrease stress, improve health, and boost happiness. Meditation is one way that people can practice mindfulness—the act of sitting quietly and clearing your thoughts can pave the way to living in the present and opening your heart and mind to what's around you, instead of ruminating, worrying, and fearing what could or has happened.

You can also use mindfulness to improve how you handle conflict. A mindful state of mind will help you (and, indirectly, the other person) focus on finding a positive way forward instead of getting bogged down in all the other noise in your head that's leading you in unhelpful directions. In his book *Full Catastrophe Living*, Kabat-Zinn outlines the key tenets of mindfulness. In terms of conflict management, these six are particularly relevant:

1. **Nonjudgment:** You, like everyone else, have ideas and opinions about basically everything. Your mind provides a steady stream of black-and-white judgments, conscious and subconscious, all day

long: like/dislike, yes/no, good/bad, etc. Being mindful means to be aware of this process, and to instead consciously hold off on judgment to allow what is unfolding to take shape. In conflicts, this helps you to be open-minded about the other person, their perspective, and solutions that you may not have considered yet.

2. **Acceptance, Letting Go, and Nonstriving:** These three attitudes focus on accepting the situation as it currently is, without forcing it to be what it is not by emotionally clinging, grasping, pushing, or pulling. This doesn't mean you cannot want something to shift. It does mean that by first accepting what it is now and not immediately wanting to do something about it, you free up a lot of headspace to allow new ways forward to emerge.

3. **Beginner's Mind:** Mindfulness encourages you to approach situations and the people involved with fresh eyes. Your mind constantly projects a ton of desires, opinions, and past hurts— some of which might be decades old—onto current situations. All of this history makes it hard to see what is actually going on right now and to recognize the potential that may be arising. Beginner's mind also benefits the other party because people feel seen and valued if you engage with how they are and what they do now, instead of how they were or got to be in your mind. This shift in mindset brings positivity and connection into disagreements, which supports finding a positive outcome.

4. **Trust:** Bringing trust into your interactions is a powerful tool. Trust starts with trusting yourself, knowing that your perspective and experience are right for you and that you can meet whatever comes at you. The more you trust yourself, the more trust you can bring to other people, to your relationships, and to handling difficult situations, because you know you have everything that's needed to bring forth a positive outcome.

5. **Patience:** In general, people are very impatient to get to what they think is the next important thing. But this attitude leads to not being in the present moment. If you rush all the time, you won't see the synchronicities and opportunities that present themselves.

6. **Gratitude and Generosity:** These mindsets bring lightheartedness, appreciation, and connection to your difficult situations. By not taking everything for granted and by giving other people opportunities to succeed, you enhance interconnection between you and the other party. Gratitude and generosity naturally foster a positive atmosphere, which every hard conversation can benefit from.

COMMON CONFLICT TERMS, MADE MINDFUL

The terms used in this book have been chosen consciously. The term "other person" is used to describe what you otherwise might call your "opponent." The word "opponent" sounds overly harsh and implies you are on opposing ends of a situation. This is often not true to begin with, but it also creates a win-lose mentality that doesn't support a mindful approach to handling difficult situations.

Given the fact that not every difficult conversation will end in a concrete solution to the problem or challenge on the table, the term "solution" is used only in specific situations. Instead, expect to find terms like "the way forward" or "conclusion" to indicate the result of a difficult conversation.

Mindfulness acknowledges that these mindsets are not something you can achieve fully overnight—but that's all right (there's the nonjudgment and patience at play!). Observing and recognizing your behavior is the first step to changing it, so that's the best place to start. Look for quick, everyday ways to practice mindfulness in your life. For example, the next time you notice yourself judging someone's cart at the grocery store, stop and notice the feeling, then let the thought go. If you find yourself angry at the slow checkout line at the store, take a few deep breaths and try to observe a few interesting things around you at that moment instead of letting the stress get to you. When you get to the front of the line, try showing genuine gratitude to the checkout employee for their hard work. Small, simple practices like this will help you make mindfulness a habit, which in turn makes it easier to access in difficult conversations.

The Positive Opportunities That Exist in Difficult Conversations

When you enter difficult conversations in a mindful way, you begin to see how much good can come out of them. When you think of conflict in a non-mindful way, however, you might find yourself focusing only on negative possibilities and aspects of such conversations, such as:

- **Fear:** Fear is a common reason people dread conflict. You might fear the emotions that may arise, fear being vulnerable, fear losing people when you express what you really think, or fear not being liked.

- **Minimization:** Often, you'll find yourself rationalizing why a difficult conversation isn't necessary: "I don't think he meant it this way" or "This is actually just a really small thing; I don't want to blow it out of proportion." This kind of reasoning leads to saying things like "I can deal with this," "I will forget about it," and "I'll just have to suck it up," which are all unhealthy things to do when you're hurt, angry, scared, or sad.

- **Stubbornness:** If you anticipate a conflict in a non-mindful way, you might start by determining what you'll refuse to give up. You might plan in advance the lines you won't cross before you hear a word the other person says.

- **Avoidance:** By avoiding a difficult conversation or that talk to finally end a conflict, you are withholding important opportunities from yourself and the other person. Most issues won't disappear on their own, and not facing them isn't doing you or the other person any favors.

Thankfully, these negative possibilities fade away when you focus on mindful practices. You'll see how fear, minimization, and stubbornness don't contribute to a successful outcome. Instead, you can open your eyes and mind to all the positive results you could enjoy, such as sharing your thoughts and feelings, connecting with the other person in a new and different way, and growing as a person. Let's take a closer look at some of these positive outcomes of mindful conflict resolution.

Everyone Can Share Their Thoughts and Feelings

The most obvious opportunity in engaging in a difficult conversation is that all participants will be able to share their perspective on things, and that together, you can try to find a way forward that satisfies everyone. This can be really worthwhile for the longer term.

It is so important to express your thoughts and feelings, even when you are not used to doing that or feel it's easier and less stressful to just ignore them. You are a crucial part of the relationship, and without your input the relationship won't be what it could be. When you decide not to share your feelings about the situation, in a one-on-one conflict this means that 50 percent of the opinions and feelings are not heard. These unexpressed opinions and feelings are not unimportant, and most of the time, they won't just "go away." They are just as relevant and valid as the opinions of the other person involved. Sucking it up or ignoring feelings is the least respectful thing to do to yourself and, ultimately, to the other person, too, because not speaking your mind will undoubtedly lead to trouble in the future. Maybe you've heard the saying: "If you don't say it, you'll show it"; that option invariably has a worse outcome. Having an honest conversation will lead to an easier, brighter future for all involved, including a possible improvement in the situation for yourself and/or the other people involved.

A NOTE ON SAFETY

If the person you're speaking with creates a violent atmosphere, there is zero chance you'll be having a successful experience. If you are in a violent situation, get out immediately. Maybe there will be another moment to resume the conversation in a safe environment.

You'll Deepen Your Relationship with the Other Person

A very important opportunity in difficult conversations is to deepen the relationship you have with the other person or people involved. Simply having a difficult conversation requires bravery, and that courage alone will strengthen the relationship because it shows the other person they are an important and valued part of your life. The fact that both of you get to share your truth with integrity and honesty will add to that connection. Telling others what you want, believe, and feel is a very openhearted thing to do, and it can be done without damaging the relationship you have with each other.

When approached mindfully, difficult conversations might not lead to that sudden breakup, the denouncing of a friendship, or that firing. On the contrary, they can strengthen your relationships thanks to the tenets of nonjudgment, acceptance, a beginner's mind, trust, patience, and gratitude and generosity.

Parties Can Experience Personal Growth

You have the opportunity to grow as a person through your initiative to start a difficult conversation mindfully. Sometimes your own faults and habits are the most difficult to see, but mindful practices can help you observe and change them in a gentle way. For example, your growth might come in the form of mustering the courage to actually have a difficult conversation, being open to several different outcomes, learning to understand why you respond the way you do, or getting to know your deeper motives or beliefs.

You Can Get to Know Each Other

Another powerful opportunity found in conflict is that you allow people to get to know you better. When you use the mindful speaking approach you'll learn in this book, you will disclose honest opinions and perspectives. In your personal life, expressing how you truly feel about something insensitive a family member said can help you and the other party learn more about each other. If you avoid that conversation, the level of openness and honesty in your relationship might drop, which, after a while, might make your connection feel shallow.

In turn, by mindfully listening to the other person's opinions and perspectives, you will get to know them better. This leads to improved understanding both ways, and probably to higher appreciation for each other and to easier future interactions.

You Can Help Others

By having difficult conversations, you can actually help other people in many different ways. This can be either a direct or an indirect result of the conversation you engage in. For example, the conversation might:

- Allow the other person to speak their truth.

- Help the other person feel appreciated, valued, and seen or heard.

- Inspire the other person to change their ineffective or harmful behavior.

- Motivate the other person to have a similar conversation with a loved one, a friend, or a colleague.

For example, if the ineffective behavior from a colleague at work impacts you, finding a mindful way to discuss this with them can help them adjust their behavior. This will influence how you two interact, and it may even improve their career.

You May Find a Way Forward That Fits Everyone's Needs

By approaching your disagreement from a mindful perspective, keeping the conversation positive, and focusing on what's happening at the present moment, solutions often arise that fit everyone's needs. In many cases, disagreement exists as a result of what people perceive—from their personal perspective—to be the only possible solution that works for them. When you're open to hearing everyone's actual needs, however, it is very possible that there are several workable outcomes in which everyone "wins." For example, it's your son's birthday, and he wants to invite all of his school friends to celebrate. You, however, want to keep your house clean, as extended family will be coming in a few days to celebrate. To make both of you "win," you could host a children's party in the park or at a local museum or gym.

Mindful Lesson: An Unexpected Outcome

Partners Bob and Shane are considering where to go on their summer vacation. Bob has his heart set on breathing in some of that beautiful European culture, so he suggests that they go to Amsterdam and London. Shane, however, really wants to soak up some sun, like in Hawaii. Bob's idea to go to these wind- and rain-prone cities really doesn't excite Shane at all.

Bob and Shane know the approach to mindful conflict resolution and know that, if they stay at the level of the "solutions" they have already come up with to have their own needs met (European cities versus Hawaii), they will probably get stuck in a very long back-and-forth where each party is argumentative. Instead, they decide to keep an open mind and talk about their underlying needs (to experience European culture versus sunbathing).

After they have both had the chance to share their needs, they quickly realize that it's not at all hard to find a place to travel to that fits what each of them wants out of their summer. They decide to explore the southern part of Europe, which has a sunny and warm climate along with a rich culture. After browsing the Internet for a bit, they find a lovely place to stay in Tuscany—a beautiful region in Italy with a lovely climate, beaches, and historically important cities like Florence and Pisa—leaving both of them happy and excited about their upcoming vacation! Instead of getting bogged down in whose idea would "win," Bob and Shane focused on listening to each other's interests and were open to outcomes they hadn't previously considered.

Entering Conflicts with Thoughtful Intention

To support your mindful attitude, it is very helpful to set a constructive intention for your conversation. An intention is a positive statement of what you want to experience or achieve. In mindful conflict resolution, your intention guides your mindset, thoughts, and actual contribution and thus influences the course of the conversation.

How to Define Intentions for Conflicts

A general guideline for setting a constructive intention is to base it on curiosity or the aim for collective success. Examples of positive and constructive intentions for mindful conflict resolution are:

- I want to gain a better understanding of the other person's perspective.
- I want to share my vision on this topic.
- I want to find a way toward mutual acceptance or agreement.

Taking a moment to define your intention is worth the effort because it will naturally put you in a mindful frame of mind as you think about the conversation. Mindful intentions also take the focus off black-or-white results and help you find a constructive, positive, and open-minded place to start from.

The Power of Intentions

Your intention has a big effect on what will happen in the conversation because the purpose behind the things you do and say has an impact both on the way you send out your message and on the way the message is received. It actually affects which words you use and how and why you use them.

You may think that your intention is your little secret, but this is in fact not true. When you speak, you send out what are called "intention cues"—subtle signals from your face, voice, and body to let the audience know the true meaning behind your words. If your cues are aligned with the actual words you speak, this leads to congruence, which signals to the other person that you can be trusted. If they are not aligned, however, it leads to confusion and distracts from your message, making it ineffective. So if you "say all the right things," but your intention is to win by having the other person admit they were wrong, you will send out mixed signals and thus be ineffective, leaving the other person confused and unsure about your trustworthiness.

THE VOICE IS THE MOST ACCURATE INDICATOR OF OUR TRUE EMOTIONS

In a 2017 study conducted at Yale University, researchers compared how well we pick up emotions from three different channels of communication: the voice, the face, and nonverbal signs. They concluded from investigating all the various scenarios (including the one where all three channels were available) that people most accurately recognize emotions in interactions where we only hear the other person's voice.

Mindful Responsibility: Taking Ownership of the Conversation

Ideally, both partners choose a mindful approach in handling their conversation, which means that they agree to the paradigm laid out in this chapter. These "ground rules" make the chance of success much higher, and if both participants work with them, you can be pretty sure a shared positive outcome will be reached.

When the Other Party Is Mindful Too

You both have "ownership" of the conversation, which means you are equal partners in the conversation, and both of you should try to make sure the conversation plays itself out in a constructive way. If the other party is naturally leaning toward mindful practices, that's wonderful! You might be able to learn new techniques from each other.

When the Other Party Isn't Cooperative

One important note: You cannot control what the other person does. So waiting for them to do the right thing isn't wise. Only you can be a sure way to the right mindset, intention, and attitude being present, so own it and set a good example!

If the other person is uncooperative, you can still positively influence the results of the conversation by staying with your mindful intention, taking ownership, and influencing the course of the conversation with your mindful attitude. Even if just one person changes their behavior, the situation changes.

It's important to realize that you cannot change the other person; you may only change the way you respond to their behavior. On the upside, if you change your response, their behavior might change as well. When, for example, your partner accuses you of never doing the dishes, you may choose a mindful response by talking about your indignation, instead of reacting directly from it: "When you say something like that, I feel attacked and handled unjustly." And maybe you may add: "But I do hear that you would appreciate me doing the dishes on a regular basis—is that right?" This might very well invite your partner into a much more constructive talk where you discuss both your needs in sharing household responsibilities.

Defining Success in Mindful Conflict Resolution

One key area where mindful conflict resolution is different from a traditional model is the outcome. When asked what they see as success in a difficult conversation, people often say things like "to have the other person admit I am right" or "getting my way." But ironically, this is not how most difficult conversations end. Most of the time, there's far too much background involved or too much future at stake for one of the participants to suddenly say that they were wrong all along, and they now want to do things exactly the way you've proposed.

In fact, when that rare occurrence does happen, on some level you probably feel that that statement won't be the end of the trouble, because it happened too easily. Maybe it will solve the problem for today, yes. But most likely there will come a moment when you'll have to revisit the topic, because that type of one-sided resolution often signals passive aggressiveness and will hardly ever be the real end of it.

That's why, in mindfully approaching difficult conversations, being told you are right will not equal success.

Move Past Winning or Losing

We live in a culture where winning versus losing is a relatively normal way to look at our interactions with other people. If you win, I must lose, and vice versa. If you get that job we are both after, I'll lose out. If your company gets that client, mine won't. And the person who wins most is the most successful. This winning versus losing mindset might get you ahead when you're trying to get the last seat on the train, that great rent-controlled place, or the presidency, but when you are in situations in which there is more at stake than just one thing to be "won" (which is most of the time!), it may be exactly what keeps you from finding a positive way forward.

PRACTICAL MINDFULNESS

Mindfully approaching your difficult conversation is the kinder thing to do, may be more aligned with your values, and may even complement the kind of person you want to be. But the truth is, mindful conflict resolution is also simply the quickest, most effective way to discover how to move forward while respecting everyone's needs.

Winning versus losing leads to a mindset of separation and wanting to beat the other person. This does anything but support a constructive debate. In most difficult conversations, you and the other person may disagree on the best way forward or why things got to be as they are right now, but you are still both kind human beings who care about the topic of conversation and who want to find the most positive way forward. The winning versus losing setup is inherently out of sync with those mindful realities.

You Can Both Be Right at the Same Time

Wanting to "beat" the other person so you can win is not a mindful, nor an effective, way to deal with difficult conversation. Having an intention like that will put your focus on finding a way to undermine what the other person is saying. At best, that may lead to you winning this particular battle, but in most cases it will lead only to endless struggle and won't end the war. And even if you do "win," what will be the collateral damage in the relationship between the two of you?

If you are able to accept from the start that both of you probably have a pretty good case for why you behaved the way you have or believe what you believe, and that you can both "win," you can get past winning or losing and start the search for what will really help you move forward. The fundamental shift to make in your mind is accepting that it's not necessary to find who is right and who is wrong, because you can both be right at the same time.

If this is true, what does success in mindful conflict resolution look like?

What Mindful Success Looks Like

When you choose a mindful approach, success can have many faces depending on the various situations you may be in, such as the following:

- **In a conversation where you need to deliver bad news**—for example, you are breaking up with your boyfriend—a great result will be when you are able to get the message across gently and kindly, handle the emotions (maybe anger, maybe sadness) that the other person is projecting, explain the reasons why, and stand your ground in a firm yet compassionate way.

- **In a disagreement about the best way forward in a difficult situation,** success will be when you find an alternative solution that everyone agrees with, or when you at least discuss the underlying needs and find a way to incorporate these in an approach both of you agree to.

- **In a long-standing conflict,** the best result may be if both of you have an opportunity to share your take on the situation and come to a place of mutual respect, even though you still don't see eye to eye in this matter.

Your best bet is to allow the things that actually happen in the conversation to lead you to the best possible outcome and not cling to desired results you've decided on beforehand. "Let that go" are very valuable words to consider in a mindful approach. Letting go of preconceived "solutions" will help you be flexible and respond to what is actually presenting itself during the conversation and work with that. This is why being present in the moment is so important.

You Can Still Get What You Want

Shifting the way you look at success in difficult conversations doesn't mean you cannot still get what you want, but you will no longer define success on that alone. Sometimes, taking on the situation in a mindful way may lead to both of you getting what you wanted to begin with, and sometimes it may lead to a situation where you do not get what you thought you wanted before you had the conversation, but you get something even better.

The success you are likely to achieve by being mindful in a difficult situation is coming to a mutual agreement about the best way forward. If you let go of that specific result you think you want and believe that the situation will be handled in a fair and just manner, you are accepting and trusting (two of the key mindfulness tenets discussed earlier in this chapter). When you allow yourself to really take in the other person's perspective in a nonjudgmental way, and you speak your truth in a sincere and open way, there may be results possible that none of the participants could have ever imagined.

Mindful Lesson: Being Open to New Solutions

Every other year, Josh and his mom, Betty, go on a mother-son trip. This year, the trip's scheduled and the plans are made, but Josh has second thoughts. His business is finally getting some traction, and he hasn't been able to spend a lot of time with his wife and their one-year-old daughter.

Josh has decided that he needs to cancel his plans with Betty, but he is really scared to tell her. He knows his mom is superexcited about the trip—plus, in the past, she's been quick to make him feel defensive about his decisions. Josh loves his mom and hates to disappoint her.

As the trip is getting closer, Josh can't postpone the discussion any longer. He finally musters the courage to talk to Betty. He sets a conscious intention to share his feelings openly and to not be pushed into a defensive mode by adopting the mindful attitudes of beginner's mind and (self-)trust.

As Josh shares his decision, Betty indeed feels disappointed. She was looking forward to spending one-on-one time with her son. And she really wanted to visit London. By practicing the attitudes of acceptance and letting go, combined with a sense of generosity, she begins to see Josh's perspective: He's working very hard to make his business sustainable, and she can only imagine the toll his new fatherhood might be taking on him. She shares this with him but adds that she would have loved to spend time together and also would have liked him to tell her sooner so she would have been able to make other plans.

Josh understands and offers his mom a heartfelt apology. He suggests that he would be able to regularly meet with her for a coffee, to catch up. Also, they could postpone the mother-son trip to later this year when he expects things to have settled down. Josh realizes suddenly that his father had mentioned wanting to travel more with Betty and suggests this as a way to have Betty make it to London. Betty calls her husband, Jim, who is delighted to be able to go and sees no problem in arranging this on short notice.

By both adopting a mindful attitude and sharing their way of seeing things without falling into accusations, Josh and Betty are open to new solutions emerging, which in the end brings forth a great option that nobody considered before.

When the Outcome Isn't Your Decision

You might sometimes experience a difficult conversation that deals with an issue you're not in a position to change. For example, let's say your boss assigned you a specific task that you really do not want. In those types of situations, it's important to realize that, even though you may not be able to change how things move forward, you can still:

- Take ownership of the conversation.
- Decide how you will handle the news.
- Control how you feel about yourself after the conversation is over.
- Influence how your relationship with the other person is affected by the conversation.

Embracing mindful attitudes like acceptance and letting go will support you in handling your emotions in a conversation where the conclusion is out of your control. Being fully present with the experience and trusting yourself will help you stay connected to what you need in order to accept what is coming at you.

In the situation where you're assigned that task you don't want to do, you might want to keep an open mind and ask for an explanation of why the assignment was given to you. Or you might want to calmly voice the irritation or hurt you're experiencing in the present moment. These techniques are not likely to change the outcome, but they will affect how you feel afterward—therefore leading to a more successful conclusion to the conversation.

Even in extremely challenging situations like a breakup or being laid off, you are still the co-owner of the outcome of the conversation. How you choose to interact has a big impact on the conversation, on the other person, and on you and how you will feel about yourself when the conversation is over.

The same goes for situations like the great rent-controlled place and the presidency, where a third party makes the decision. Even though the decision on how to move forward is out of your hands, you can still have a personal impact on how the conversation evolves. Always remember: You have a responsibility to influence the conversation for the better by bringing in a mindful attitude, and if you do, the results will reflect that. If one person changes, the situation changes.

The mindful approach may not always lead to a shared success, but it will lead to you getting out with your integrity and dignity intact. In situations where the outcome is not up to you, you may have to accept that "success" is that you shared your perspective on the matter and kept the conversation out of fighting or accusation mode.

CHAPTER SUMMARY

The following are takeaways, action steps, and reminders to help you progress smoothly into mindful conflict resolution.

● The key attitudes that create mindful awareness are nonjudgment, acceptance, beginner's mind, trust, patience, and gratitude and generosity.

● By setting a constructive intention for the conflict, you will further influence the conversation positively.

● Mindful conflict resolution is not only the kinder, more compassionate way to deal with difficult conversations, disagreements, and conflicts—it is also the quickest, most effective way to discover how to move forward while respecting everyone's needs.

● Engaging in difficult conversations offers valuable opportunities, such as the chance to share your truth and the opportunity to grow and improve yourself and to help the other person do so as well. But the most important reason not to shy away from having a difficult conversation is the chance to deepen the bond between the two of you.

● To adopt a mindful approach, you need to move away from the win-lose mentality. Winning won't really get you what you want, as it will lead to revisiting the topic later, or a damaged relationship.

● Being successful looks different now that you're approaching things in a mindful way. Success may be, depending on the situation, finding an unexpected way forward that respects everyone's needs, seeing and appreciating everyone's perspective, or sharing your own take on things with dignity.

CHAPTER 2
THE POWER OF INTERCONNECTION

"Recognize that the other person is you."

Yogi Bhajan

Conflicts and difficult conversations can easily set up a belief that it's basically you against the rest of the world. You might tell yourself that other people are out to get you and want you to fail or lose out. But in mindful conflict management, you'll instead find and appreciate the connections all people share. The truth is that all people want to be happy, feel safe, and avoid suffering. To some degree we are perfectly aware of this shared human need. But it is such an obvious premise that it's also easily forgotten. In this chapter, you will learn how to make this important shift in perspective to seeing the other party as a fellow human with similar basic needs, which will help you connect to people in a way that is probably different from what you are now used to. Interconnection—the ability to recognize your own needs and the other person's simultaneously—is the foundation on which mindful conflict resolution rests. You will quickly see how interconnection can support you in working toward conclusions that address everyone's needs.

How People Usually Approach Communication

First, let's explore the most common approaches people take when interacting with others and why none of these support a mindful way of working through difficult conversations.

The Objective Approach: Facts, Facts, Facts

You've probably noticed how most people are very focused on getting the facts straight. They focus on the objective side of things and try to get a clear and complete scope of what is going on. In a disagreement, they will want to know exactly how things happened, and what the rationale behind the decisions has been. This method can help them get their heads around the situation.

When all the information is on the table, they will then have an objective look at things and try to solve the conflict by first finding what is truest for most people. Content seems indisputable, so when there's disagreement, there's apparently information missing. They think that gathering more information will eventually lead to complete and clear information, which in turn will lead to clear solutions.

The "My Story" Approach: Telling Your Side

Some people who focus on facts are primarily focused on wanting to get their own view of what happened or what is happening across to the other people involved. They explain their own perspective, sending out what they know, and may try to persuade the other person to see things their way.

The "Your Story" Approach: Finding Out What the Other Person Knows

Others are very interested in figuring out how the other person sees things. They ask a ton of questions to clarify the other person's perspective. What information do they have? What opinions have they formed? What do they know?

They believe that gathering this information leads to transparency and a level playing field, which is great. In situations where there is a straightforward disagreement, that might be enough to solve it by making a rational decision.

The Problem with These Approaches: They Don't Go Deep Enough to Reach a Conclusion

You have probably been in situations where all the facts were on the table and everyone had told their "side," yet there wasn't a clear solution. The thing is, in most difficult conversations, neither the real problem nor the solution lies in the facts or each person's story. Focusing on content may get you to an objective "solution," but in a difficult situation, that will probably not satisfy everyone involved. In those situations, the problem usually exists because people do not interpret the facts in the same way (the he said–she said dilemma). In other cases, emotions or experiences make it impossible to straightforwardly "solve" the problem in a rational way.

The Mindful Approach: Feelings and Connection

Neither of these approaches is usually successful. The underlying motives and beliefs of both participants are left out, which makes reaching a sustainable solution highly improbable. No matter how challenging the conflict, it's important to be open to hearing how the other person sees things. In order to find a way forward that works for everyone, you'll need to invite subjective information about feelings, emotions, beliefs—in short, "the inner world"—to come into the discussion. To really understand what is going on, both for yourself and the other person, it is important to learn to explore the inner worlds of all people involved. To be able to mindfully handle difficult situations, it is always necessary to move beyond the contents of the discussion and connect as humans.

If it's your natural tendency to focus on content, this chapter invites you to take a pretty big leap, which may require practice and time. Be compassionate with yourself, and just begin by exploring your own motives behind how you choose to present and interpret facts.

Dipping a Toe Into Connection: My World versus Your World

When you start to explore the inner world, beyond facts and stories, there are different ways to do this. One way is to be deeply connected with your own inner world; the other is to be focused on what the other person wants.

My World

People who focus on their own world:

- Are primarily in tune with how they feel about things.

- Trust and value their own opinion.

- Can articulate what they need and want in challenging situations.

When others offer them their perspective, they focus specifically on where that perspective differs from or complements their own view, and they focus their response on how that makes them feel or what they want next. You could say they are focused on getting what they want. Furthermore, if they believe other people are more or less the same as them, they therefore expect the other person to take care of themselves, too, thus creating a level playing field in the conversation.

Your World

On the other hand, some people are primarily focused on what other people need to feel good. They are often very well attuned to other people's energy, like empaths and highly sensitive people. When these people are in a conversation with someone else, they usually:

- Listen deeply to what the other person wants, often hearing more than is actually being said.

- Do everything in their power to let the other person leave happy.

- Try to avoid conflicts and difficult conversations as much as they can.

- Want to resolve conflicts as soon as possible; this will often lead to quick solutions without them really checking within themselves if this would be okay for them.

CHECK IT!

If you are a person who is closely attuned to other people's needs and picks up on information that is not actually being said, please do not forget to ask the other person if you are correct in your assumptions. The reason is threefold: (a) you can make mistakes, (b) it's kind, and (c) it is more helpful and more effective to let the other person decide the interpretation of the information you've sensed than to draw your own conclusions in silence.

Neither of These Approaches
Leads to Mindful Communication

After reading about these different approaches to communication, you've probably recognized your own preferred style. And maybe you're judging yourself about where you are right now. This is absolutely unnecessary, because

1. Mindfulness encourages nonjudgment.

2. Neither of these inner world mindsets will lead you to mindful conflict resolution.

Whether you're more likely to lean toward "my world" or "your world," the other, equally fundamental, perspective is left out.

- People who are well attuned to their own world ignore the need of the other person to be heard and to be acknowledged by them. Their drive to take care of their own feelings and motives means the other person's drives are easily overlooked. That will create an atmosphere of disconnection, making it harder to find common ground and a way forward that is acceptable to both of you.

- People who focus on other people first leave out their own position in the disagreement. Their wish to solve the conflict quickly and to make the other person happy leads to not being fully open about what they need or want out of the discussion. This will lead to solutions that may be temporarily okay, especially because the horror of conflict is averted, but will in the longer run probably not eradicate their reasons for disagreeing in the first place, as their position wasn't really taken into account when coming up with the solution.

That's why neither one of these approaches is ultimately successful. You will either lose connection with the other person because you are so focused on your own stance, which makes it harder or even impossible to end the conversation in a way that feels good to both parties, or you will lose connection with yourself, as being so focused on what the other person needs makes you less aware of what you need. You may be able to end the conflict, but on what terms? Instead, look to the power of interconnection to bring you both together.

What Is Interconnection?

The crucial first skill to develop to resolve conflicts and disagreements in a mindful way is to bring the "me" and "you" approaches together—to learn to be connected to yourself, and from that connection to self, reach out and connect with the other person. This is called "interconnection."

Let's circle back to that deceptively simple premise discussed at the beginning of this chapter: All people basically want the same thing, namely to be happy, feel secure, and avoid suffering. Fully appreciating this brings forth a feeling of compassion for all people, which means that you're kind and patient, free from judgment, and open to understand and empathize. Directing compassion toward both the other person and yourself—interconnection—is an indispensable way to mindfully handle difficult situations.

Though it sounds lovely in theory, this premise isn't always easy to implement for various reasons:

- For people who primarily work from their connection to self, it will be challenging to see the other person with that kind of compassion.

- For people who primarily work from their connection to other people, it will be challenging to appreciate that they themselves deserve that deep compassion and understanding too.

- For people who primarily focus on facts and stories, it will be challenging to have to bring in subjective content as an essential element to finding a way out of conflict.

Even if interconnection doesn't come easily to you at first, it's well worth the effort. Read on to understand how to implement this strategy.

Practicing Interconnection

Interconnecting is a skill you can use in every interaction you have with other people, preferably before it even has the chance of being difficult or turning into conflict. Follow these simple steps to start incorporating interconnection into your everyday life.

Step 1: Accept That Both Parties Can Be Right

The crucial first step to take toward interconnection is to rethink your general perception about disagreements. Interconnection requires you to fully appreciate that both parties can be equally right at the same time. This principle works from the acknowledgment that because people have different perspectives, motives, and beliefs, different truths can coexist.

Mindful Lesson:
You Are Right, and I Am Right

Imagine this: You have been living in a big city your entire life. You love how you're able to go to dinner at a different restaurant every week; you love how you can go see a movie at a moment's notice. You love how there are always people in the street, whatever time it is.

But then there's your sister. She had lived in that same big city for a large part of her life, too, but a couple of years ago, she and her partner decided to move to the country. At any family gathering, she goes on and on about the perks of living in the country: The air is so fresh, there's so much space for the children to play outside, and it's so safe. And she especially loves the peace and quiet and not seeing people all the time. Her so-called advantages of living outside the city irritate you immensely, and you dive in to counter her beliefs.

It's easy to see how that will be a difficult conversation! But you probably understand how the conflict between you and your sister does not have that much to do with being right or wrong, but stems from personal likes and dislikes. You can both be very right about the advantages you see to living where you live.

In the disconnect between you and your sister is an invitation to talk about why you love living in the city and she loves the country, because through that discussion your bond and mutual understanding may deepen.

The "You Are Right, and I Am Right" example might seem like a pretty mild conflict, but the exact same theory is true for other disagreements. Think about discussions about politics or discussing your choice of partner with your parents: They may disapprove for reasons that are relevant to them, but you make certain decisions nonetheless because of your beliefs or preferences. Who's "right" and who's "wrong" is really not what these type of conversations are about—they are actually about why one person believes one thing and the other believes something else entirely. The way forward is not in getting the facts straight but in understanding and accepting the reasons and needs behind the "facts."

The And Stance

Douglas Stone, Bruce Patton, and Sheila Heen termed the mindset of knowing that both parties in a conflict, disagreement, or difficult conversation can be right at the same time the "And Stance" in their book, *Difficult Conversations: How to Discuss What Matters Most*. Here are some examples: "You are right, and I am right." "You are tired after a rough day, and I want to go out for drinks." "You feel underappreciated, and I believe I did everything in my power to show you you are not."

Even though the And Stance might seem simple, in our deepest conflicts and our most painful conversations, people tend to completely forget "and" and instead use "but" in every thought and sentence. Instead of asking, "You love the forest trails, but did you ever think of ticks?!" you could be saying, "You love the forest trails, and please remember to use a spray against ticks."

Shifting your mindset toward the And Stance takes practice, so remind yourself again and again. Soon enough, it will be second nature to find the "and" instead of the "but."

BUILD CONNECTION WITH METTA MEDITATION

Research has long demonstrated the power of metta meditation, or loving-kindness meditation, to improve your ability to respond compassionately to yourself and others and to feel happier overall. Metta meditation is a simple practice of clearing your mind and directing well-wishes toward yourself and other people. Regular metta meditation is a great way to integrate the And Stance into your everyday life. You can find guided metta meditations online or in meditation apps (see the Online Resources section at the back of this book for some ideas).

Step 2: Connect to Yourself

The second step in the interconnection process is to connect to yourself. Independent of your current focus on self or others, this second step will probably be a little different from what you're used to. Connecting to yourself in the way that supports interconnection is not the same as knowing your position in a difficult conversation and being true to that, no matter what happens.

Connecting to yourself in interconnection is to be aware of your opinion regarding the topic and the other person in the present moment. When approaching a difficult conversation with a mindful attitude, you are open to the fact that what is true for you may evolve during the conversation you are having as you honestly take into account the contribution of the other person.

Things May Change

If you refuse to stray from whatever you think before you start a conversation, you are neglecting what is happening during your interaction. The mindful approach requires you to take in what the other person says, take in what you experience, and allow your position to evolve with that. Being connected to yourself in this sense means to constantly be consciously aware of that shifting in your opinion and how you feel, and to include everything you are gathering in what you say next.

This means that you may think X about topic A at the moment you enter the conversation, and after you have been talking for a while and have heard the other person's point of view and you experience how your conversation is evolving, your belief is gradually shifting toward Y. In any given moment, you are taking the actual exchange you are having into account when deciding your position.

Needing to Be Present

Being able to connect to yourself in this way requires you to be fully present in the moment and in your body. The simplest way to make sure you are connected to your body is to take a couple of deep abdominal breaths. Breathing will help center you, and with that type of centering comes connection to self.

ABDOMINAL, OR DIAPHRAGMATIC, BREATHING

When you breathe deeply, as deeply as you can, where in your body do you feel it? You might think it's your chest, but it's actually your abdomen—your chest doesn't need to move much at all. (See the Online Resources section at the back of this book for a short how-to video.)

Feeling What You Experience Now

Abdominal breathing is a direct way into your current feelings. It calms you down instantly, lowers your blood pressure, and encourages you to clear your mind as your focus shifts to what would otherwise be a thoughtless task—breathing. Plus, as the term "gut feeling" implies, focusing on your belly breathing signals you to take stock of your current physical state and your mental response to what is going on in and around you.

So even though your ideas technically surface in your mind, and you may have a habit of first considering what you think of something, being able to feel your body (and specifically your belly) connects you to your experience right here, right now.

When you become aware of your experience in the here and now, it's just a small step to becoming aware of the effect the other person's reasoning has on you and on your position toward the subject you are talking about. This technique of looking inward and then outward creates the type of connection to self we are after in interconnection.

KNOW WHAT'S YOURS

Another benefit of establishing a firm connection to yourself is that it is easier to distinguish between your own feelings and those of the other person. If you often find yourself absorbing other people's energy, moods, or opinions without realizing it, making this distinction is important.

Losing the Connection to Yourself Leads to Disconnection from the World

We've all had one of those days when everything seems to go wrong: Your shirt has a stain, someone cuts you off in traffic, the store clerk is rude, and it starts pouring during your walk. What does that have to do with connecting to yourself? Consider the possibility that these bad days start with you waking up disconnected from yourself and not taking the time and effort to reestablish that connection.

When you leave your own house and mingle with other people, one pillar of interconnection is already missing. And because you don't really value yourself enough that day, you will find confirmation of your unspoken premise that everyone is against you everywhere. People are unkind, nobody is giving you a break, and even Mother Nature seems to have it in for you. Instead of being in an energy of interconnection, you fall back into believing that it is you against the world.

When you are in a "me against the world" frame of mind, you start expecting other people to go out of their way to connect to you. Unfortunately, no one can do that, because you are walking around wearing a huge "protective" armor to shield yourself against the big, bad world. And when you wear that armor, people will defer to it.

You wear the armor to keep bad stuff out, but it's actually keeping all the good stuff away from you as well.

The beauty is that, once you realize how this dynamic works, you can turn it around. If you do take the time to reconnect to yourself and open up to the world and the possibility of interconnection with the people you meet, you'll experience that this works exactly the same the other way around: Practicing interconnection creates interconnection. If you give it, you'll receive it. By establishing the connection to yourself, you lower that protective shield, and by doing that, you are open to noticing the rainbow in the sky and the friendly guy letting you cut in front of him in the grocery store.

Step 3: Connect to the Other Person

Now that you are connected to yourself, it's time to open up to the person you are having the conversation with. For some people, that's not hard at all. Empaths and highly sensitive people, for example, are used to expanding their energy out toward other people and connecting with them on an energetic level. Connecting with the other person naturally leads you to trying to understand where they are coming from. You do this by:

1. Providing a safe and open space for them to share their full perspective on the matter at hand.

2. Trying to pick up more from their story than they actually put into words by being mindful of their body language and tone of voice and the overall vibe you pick up from them.

HOLD OFF ON PREPARING YOUR OWN CONTRIBUTION

In mindful conflict resolution, you should suspend thinking about and preparing your own response until the moment when you actually need to speak. That way, while the other person is sharing their story, you have all the time in the world to completely focus on them and truly listen to and understand what they're saying. Your focus should be on really trying to understand where the other person is coming from, not preparing your rebuttal. One way to keep yourself focused on the other person is to imagine yourself in their position. Be curious about what things are like for them.

Step 4: Put It All Together

Maybe the most challenging part of interconnection is simultaneously connecting to self and the other person. If you can make yourself be fully present in the moment—without being distracted by thoughts about the past or future—you will be amazed at how much extra time opens up. You can use that extra time to connect with yourself and the other person.

The Monkey Mind

There is actually a lot more time available in conversations than we normally perceive. Without a mindful approach, this time is unwittingly consumed by thinking about things that are often not going to help achieve a positive outcome to the disagreement. Our "monkey mind" chatter might be judging the other person, ourselves, or the situation; coming up with ways to win the argument; or maybe even going off topic and making grocery lists. The monkey mind is a Buddhist concept that refers to the part of our brain that is constantly chattering and giving opinions. All of this chatter is completely unhelpful— and extremely mind-consuming. By consciously practicing being aware in the moment, by feeling your body and sensing what is going on in and around you, you can notice and gently try to dismiss this type of unnecessary chatter. Then you'll open up time and space in your brain for ideas and techniques that are helpful to achieving success in your difficult conversation. (Chapter 5 will explore more deeply how to listen and be present in a conversation. For now, just become aware of your thoughts while you are "listening" to the other person explain their point of view.)

Balancing the Two Viewpoints

With interconnection, you'll approach the other person's position and your own position as equally valuable. For some people, this means that they will have to make the other person's position more important than they do now. Others will have to make their own position more important than they do now. We need both perspectives on the situation to come to a solution or a way forward that does justice to both parties. If you value one over the other, there's a big chance that the end of the conversation will actually just be the start of a new (lingering) disagreement.

How to Deal with People Who Are Difficult to Connect To

After learning about what it takes to interconnect, you might have immediately thought of a couple of people you just can't imagine connecting with in that way. Everyone has at least a few people in their life with whom it seems impossible to forge a deep connection—with whom every interaction becomes difficult because there just seems to be a mismatch in personalities.

Core Qualities and How People React to Them

Internationally acclaimed business consultant Daniel Ofman offers a straightforward model in his book *Core Qualities: A Gateway to Human Resources*. He shows that every person has a couple of qualities that are so deeply ingrained in them that they don't even see them as something special. Other people do, though. For example, think of that friend who always has time and energy to help others—her helpfulness may be her core quality. Or your brother, who always knows exactly what to say to steer attention away from himself—his modesty might be one of his core qualities.

When someone overdoes their core quality, however, that quality can turn into their pitfall. A pitfall is "too much of a good thing," and it turns the strength into a weakness. For example, helpfulness becomes meddling, careful becomes fussy, and modesty becomes invisibility.

A challenge is the positive opposite of a pitfall—it is what you have to learn. Pitfalls and challenges are complementary qualities. The objective is to strike a balance between the two. For example, it is not necessary for someone to become less decisive, but they should instead develop more patience, resulting in a patient decisiveness without nagging. For a person who has helpfulness as a core quality, it's really important to balance giving with being able to receive. Your modest brother should learn to talk in a sincere way about his talents.

The opposite of your challenge is where you'll find those people you cannot seem to connect with. People tend to respond in an "allergic" way to people who display too much of their challenge, which is basically the opposite of their core quality. These people, in turn, are acting out the pitfall to their core quality. So your helpful friend will probably be "allergic" to your other friend, who has a tendency to wait until others come to rescue him. Your modest brother will be "allergic" to his arrogant colleague, who is always tooting his own horn.

Working with Your "Allergies"

The people you feel "allergic" to are those people you respond to in an opposing, often quite emotional, way. It's not hard to see how challenging it will be to create interconnection with them: When you encounter an "allergy," a natural response is to close off and avoid it. But the truth is, as difficult as it is to imagine, these people can be your most influential teachers. Exactly where they annoy you so much is where you are challenged to expand and learn. They are displaying an exaggerated version of your challenge, making it very clear what you could develop to balance your core quality. So, for example, your modest brother is challenged to be a little more outspoken about his talents. Also, quite often, it'll be vice versa: If you are not yet balanced in your core quality, you are probably acting in a way others are absolutely "allergic" to.

Given that to be able to solve your conflicts mindfully it's necessary to remember each person's humanity and to interconnect with them, it's helpful to consider what you could learn from that obnoxious behavior you're so "allergic" to. You may even create a win-win scenario, where both of you could balance out your core qualities, which would make the interaction easier for everyone involved. This type of deep human connection and potential for mutual growth is why interconnection is so powerful and effective.

CHAPTER SUMMARY

The following are takeaways, action steps, and reminders to help you progress smoothly into mindful conflict resolution.

- Interconnection means you approach the other person's needs and your own needs in a conversation as equally valuable, and that you are compassionate toward both. Interconnection is the foundation on which mindful conflict resolution rests.

- Some people tend to naturally focus on the content of a conversation; some people care more about the feelings involved. Some are more prone to tend to their own needs, and some tend to the needs of others first. To evaluate where you are starting your journey into interconnection, first assess: Which one of these mindsets best describes you right now?

- To practice interconnection, first be prepared to accept that both you and the other person can be right. Then connect to self, stretch your energy out to the person, and hold that dual connection. By being present in the moment without engaging in your own monkey mind chatter, you have plenty of brainpower to be with yourself and the other person at the same time.

- When you start developing interconnection, you will probably move in and out of interconnection and regularly fall back into your preferred style. Practice shifting your mindset by recognizing that the other person basically wants the same things as you: to feel happy and safe and to avoid suffering.

- If interconnection is particularly difficult with a specific person, it may be because they are displaying an exaggerated version of a behavior that you should develop to bring balance to your core qualities. They are actually teaching you something, and you could teach them something as well.

CHAPTER 3
THE MANY LAYERS
WITHIN A CONVERSATION

"It's our challenges and obstacles that give us layers of depth and make us interesting. Are they fun when they happen? No. But they are what make us unique."

Ellen DeGeneres

This chapter will explore the different levels on which communication plays itself out—both what's being said and what's not being said. Being aware of these different levels will make you understand how it's possible that even though you think a conversation is about your dinner plans for next week, your partner is actually talking about your feelings about his mother.

You will learn how the things you do and do not share about yourself can make conversations difficult. This will uncover a treasure trove of information both within yourself and the other person. You will learn how to work with these layers and bring some of the information available there into the actual conversation.

What's Beneath the Surface

Some conversations are logistically difficult because the participants disagree about the facts or the best solution to the problem. Other conversations get emotionally challenging when there is a gap between what is being said and what is being thought or experienced. Let's explore a concrete situation to make this idea a bit more tangible.

Harry and Beth have been together for a couple of years. On Saturday morning, they make a meal plan for the upcoming week and an accompanying grocery list. Since they love to invite people for dinner, they also discuss whom to invite for dinner next week. They have been working on the meal plan and the list for quite some time already when the conversation turns to who's coming for dinner.

Harry: "Let's invite my mom. It's been such a long time since we've seen her."

Beth: "Mmm, I'm not sure about that... I was thinking we should invite Susan. It's been such a horrible time for her since Mark left her."

Harry: "It seems to me that you are avoiding seeing my mother. You've been doing that for months now."

Beth: "I just feel that Susan needs our support more right now."

Harry: "You're trying to make this about Susan, but it is so clear you don't want to see my mom! Do you even like her?"

Beth: "I do! Although I do find her a little controlling..."

Harry: "You see? You have a problem with my mom!"

What is happening here? At first it seems Harry and Beth are talking about dinner plans, but pretty soon the conversation takes a painful turn when Beth's relationship with Harry's mother is put under the magnifying glass. This is not an uncommon way for conversations to spin out of control. What's being said, what's not being said, and the emotions behind the words are all at play.

The Four Layers of Communication

To understand what may be going on here, let's have a look at the four levels on which our communication takes place.

1. Content

The first and most basic level of communication is content. Content is the actual topic of conversation—facts, figures, and everything provable. This is where you will discuss that grocery list and the meal plan for the week.

The questions on this level are most often simple questions that begin with the words "who," "what," "how," or "when:" "What will we be eating on Tuesday? Who's coming for dinner on the weekend? When will we go to the store?"

On this level, summarizing is a very helpful tool to keep everyone on the same page: "So far we've agreed we'll be having Indian curry on Tuesday and to ask my mom to come to dinner on Saturday."

Many people feel very much at home at the level of content because we deal with it every day. Most of the time, the facts speak for themselves, and it is clear to all participants what you are talking about. If that's not the case, it might be because the participants haven't shared the necessary information. To get clear about this, there are a couple of relevant questions to ask all parties:

- Does everyone agree on the actual subject of conversation?

- Does everyone have the same facts?

If the answer to either of these questions is negative, it's usually pretty simple to bring everyone up to speed by exchanging information and defining the topic of conversation.

2. Procedure

The procedural level of communication is characterized by how you approach the conversation, how you will discuss what you want to discuss. Relevant at this level are subjects like:

- Is everyone on the same page as to the order in which you will discuss the topic(s)?

- Does everyone agree about the amount of time you have to talk?

At work, these agreements are often pretty straightforward, such as when you send a colleague an Outlook meeting invitation and attach an agenda. In private conversations, however, there's not going to be a meeting invitation and agenda to discuss that grocery list. Despite that, you can still clarify procedural points aloud: "Let's first discuss what we are going to eat, and then we'll make a list of stuff we need to buy" or "Let's both take thirty minutes to come up with some recipes we want to eat this week."

Procedure is the first level people turn to when they don't reach a positive outcome in a conversation quickly. In the example of Harry, Beth, and their grocery list, if they are unstructured throughout the content level, simultaneously naming random things to put on the list, coming up with meal suggestions, and suggesting whom to eat with all at the same time, they are likely to encounter misunderstandings, confusion, and irritation. A procedural intervention would be to make a suggestion on how to approach the conversation about the grocery list instead of being directly drawn into the content.

3. Interaction

The interaction level is where you shift to a less tangible form of communication. For many people, it's also more intimidating and unfamiliar. Interaction refers to how you approach each other. In any conversation there are usually unwritten rules about that, such as letting each other finish their sentences, listening to each other, and making eye contact regularly.

If you run into problems in a conversation, and it's not because of content or procedure, the next thing is to explore if you have the same perspective on how the interaction should be. If you don't, it can be helpful to both parties if you outline the "rules" and make sure you both agree on them. An intervention on this level could be to suggest a different way of interacting: "Let's hear each other out" or "It's okay to discuss this topic from a personal perspective."

4. Emotion

This fourth level might seem pretty straightforward: It's about feelings and emotions. Beyond that, this level also covers the feelings and emotions you have about:

- The other person.
- Yourself.
- Your current situation.
- Your past.
- Your future.
- Your current, past, and future situations in relation to the other person.
- The thoughts you have about your feelings and emotions and what they mean.

Your feelings and emotions are based on your beliefs and opinions about yourself, the other person, and the situation. It's easy to see how this is the layer where the true complication of difficult conversations arises. Not only do you experience this, but the other person does as well. That's a lot of emotions to process.

People Often Hide Their Feelings

One challenge within this layer is that sometimes people aren't very explicit and open about what they feel. They usually end up showing how they feel eventually, but the information comes out in an unproductive and sometimes hurtful way. When discussing whom to invite for dinner on Saturday, this is the level where things go wrong when you suggest inviting your best friend instead of your partner's mother. Rather than responding with a rational "yes" or "no," your partner may launch into a tantrum about how you never liked his mother in the first place, leaving you to feel confused and clueless as to what really happened. What happened is that emotions and feelings came into play.

Intervening on this level requires awareness of yourself and the other person—and courage. An intervention would be to say something like "I see you are angry" and wait for the response.

Challenges upon Challenges

In the example of the grocery list-making couple, obstacles are everywhere: the need to decide what to eat, when, and with whom—while requiring the navigation of challenges on the levels of procedure, interaction, and emotion. All of these variables create plenty of ways for the conversation to become difficult.

THE INTERACTION AND EMOTION LEVELS HAVE THE MOST POTENTIAL FOR IMPROVEMENT

Many situations are dealt with at the levels of content and procedure, because this is where people feel safe and capable. Many people avoid the interaction and the emotion levels, as they fear being sucked into a conversation they do not know how to handle—for example, because they don't know how to deal with emotions. But on these levels are some really relevant opportunities that, when used well, deepen the conversation and may even solve disagreement. Plus, if whatever is going on in interaction and emotion are out in the open and dealt with in a healthy way, content and procedure will more or less take care of themselves.

On top of the challenges already discussed at each of the levels, one of the biggest hiccups can occur when one party experiences a challenge on one level while the other party experiences a whole different challenge on another level. For example, while one person is talking about content, the other person may on a superficial level seem to be talking about that same content, but actually is being confronted with surfacing anger (emotion level) or a feeling that they are not being taken seriously (interaction level).

Mind the (Conversation) Gap

Given the presence of multiple layers of conversations, it's easy to see how gaps between levels can occur easily—meaning gaps between what is being said and what is being thought or experienced. This gap can occur on any of the four levels of a conversation.

Content and Procedure Levels

On the content and procedure levels, the gap arises when people don't agree on the topic, the facts, or the procedure on how to approach the discussion. While this situation certainly happens quite a lot, the solution is not too complicated. Most often, one of the participants will come to realize the misalignment and call it out.

Misalignment within the content and procedure levels can easily be prevented or cured by being transparent about your own assumptions regarding the topic, facts, and procedure. You can just quickly check in about these points at the beginning of the conversation. As soon as you realize there's a misconception, you can take the lead in closing the gap. For example, you may believe you and your friend are discussing next weekend's plans, and you suddenly realize he is talking about the weekend after that. Or at work, you may realize your one-on-one with your boss doesn't leave enough time to thoroughly discuss the proposal you've prepared, so instead you make an appointment for later in the week so you will both have time and dedicated attention to go over it.

Interaction and Emotion Levels

Simple solutions are harder to find on the third and fourth levels. The third level is where inexperience becomes a factor, because most people are not used to talking about the "rules" of the way we interact and discuss topics. Most of these "rules" are unwritten and undiscussed, so people don't even know what they're missing.

The fourth level is also an area of inexperience; plus, for many people, it's an area they consciously prefer to stay away from. Some people might even be a little afraid of what could happen on this level. Emotions have a bad reputation in difficult conversations, because they can seem unpredictable and out of our control. Discussing things on the emotion level brings up uncertainty for many of us, and uncertainty in this case often leads to wanting to avoid it altogether.

Mindful Lesson:
Working with Different Conversation Levels

Sebastian and Frank are good friends. When they go out for a drink one night, Sebastian tells Frank about his struggles at work. His colleagues have different standards and work ethics from him, and the environment is becoming very political. While he's telling Frank about it, his tone becomes quite agitated. His face reddens. Frank is surprised and a little worried. He doesn't usually see Sebastian in such a state.

To show his support, Frank starts asking a lot of questions about what happened and when. While Sebastian answers them, Frank is aware that his friend isn't getting any less upset—on the contrary! He soon realizes that he's not really helping Sebastian by asking him all these content-related questions. Sebastian is clearly very emotional, so Frank needs to move to that level of conversation.

Frank says: "Seb, I am sorry; I only now realize that this is probably bigger than who said what. You're clearly very upset about the company culture. Is it okay to talk about that instead?" When Sebastian confirms, Frank says: "I see you're really mad about how they are treating you. It sounds like the atmosphere in your office is deteriorating—is that right? You look pretty pissed."

With those words, Frank brings the conversation to an interaction and emotion level. Sebastian feels heard and acknowledged, and as a result he allows himself to dive deeper into his feelings about what is going on.

By talking through his feelings about his colleagues' actions, Sebastian comes to terms with the fact that the office culture is touching him on a level beyond his professional opinions—it is clashing with his core values. He becomes more and more aware that this company's common practices don't align with his values, and he starts to consider his future in the organization. At the end of the talk, both Sebastian and Frank feel grateful for the connection they were able to establish in this conversation and the clarity that Sebastian gained from it.

The Layers in People: We Are All Icebergs

Now that you know how the four levels of communication can complicate your conversations, let's take it a step further and think about what we can learn about the actual people engaging in a conversation.

As you think about how people handle difficult conversations, consider this: You are an iceberg, not because of being cold and frozen, but because of how much you share with other people about yourself. Harvard University psychologist David McClelland stated that, like an iceberg, most people show only the tip of who they truly are to others. Of course, this depends on your personal preferences and how well you know the other person—but still, our deepest motivations are often known to no one (not even ourselves).

As a kid, you probably were pretty open about your feelings, emotions, motives, and beliefs. Then as you grew up, you learned to hide a lot of this to be polite, to be liked, to fit in, etc. McClelland determined that people end up showing (through their behavior and the things they say) as little as 10 percent of who they really are. The other 90 percent is hidden below the waterline of the huge iceberg you have become.

Icebergs are so important to difficult conversations because that 90 percent of you that's "hidden" is actually very relevant to whatever you are talking about. It influences your behavior even though you may often be unaware of it. This explains why some people will respond in a highly emotional way to something that doesn't affect someone else at all—something, like an old experience or a deep-seated belief about how things should be, triggers the emotional outburst, while in the other person, this experience or belief is absent and thus will not be triggered.

The Layers of the Iceberg

Your personal iceberg contains three different layers:

1. The first layer is the 10 percent of what you do show to others, and it consists of your knowledge, skills, and behavior (this is the level of your doing).

2. The second layer is right below the waterline and consists of what you think about others and what you think about yourself. Here are your norms, beliefs, and values. Also, this is where you find your self-image (this is the level of your thinking).

3. The third layer is deeper down in the iceberg and consists of your personality traits and the deep motives that drive you (this is the level of your wanting).

Ideally, you would at least know all the parts of your own iceberg. But unfortunately, many people are not yet in touch with their layers.

Then, when difficult topics surface, they are as surprised by their deepest beliefs, fears, and motives popping up as other people are.

How to Identify and Handle the Deep Layers of Your Iceberg

Learning about your own deeper layers is one of the most powerful steps you can take to become more mindful and compassionate and less reactive. Personal development—the process of improving your self-awareness, self-knowledge, and self-esteem, possibly with the help of a coach or therapist—will help you to form a clearer idea of your norms, beliefs, values, and self-image (second layer) and your deepest motives and drivers (third layer). The exploration of these deeper layers takes time, probably a lifetime, so don't feel like you have to wait until you master the subject to start practicing it. The more you know, the easier it gets, though, so starting on personal development today is a good idea.

BUT WHY?

An amazingly simple way to start exploring your own underlying motives and beliefs is to ask yourself "Why?"—not once, but several times about various topics and situations. You can practice this around challenging topics, such as when you prepare to enter into a difficult conversation. With each "Why?" you'll go a level deeper, and with your honest answer comes a deeper understanding of yourself.

The more you push down or close your eyes to whatever you have in your second and third iceberg layers, the more uncontrollable and unexpected the emotions become. Think of beach balls (icebergs and beach balls might seem incongruous, but stay with me). They are fun to throw around, and their lightness makes them easy to handle even for the smallest hands. But when you take them into the water and try to push them under, they become uncontrollable. They don't want to stay under, and they pop up randomly in the least expected places.

This is the same with the feelings inside our deeper layers. They pop up as emotions that start to handle you, instead of you handling them. They may pop up in the conversation you are having at work, or later, at home for example, where they express themselves as a short fuse when your partner or child asks you something. Like beach balls, the deeper aspects of your personality are not meant to be pushed down, but they should be allowed to be colorful and bright and out in the open.

It's much easier to learn how to deal with your deep beliefs and motives when you allow them to be visible to yourself and others than when you try to keep them out of sight. But unfortunately, most people haven't really learned how to do that in a sincere, yet "semidetached," way, meaning you would allow your feelings to be present without having them capture you in an emotional outburst. To clarify this, just imagine being in a difficult conversation with your partner. They have been coming home late a couple of days in a row, and you are getting anxious about them not being so in love with you anymore. This anxiety may be stemming from the deep belief that you need their love to be okay. These are probably not the types of emotions and beliefs that you are proudest of, and maybe you would want to keep them out of sight when you're discussing what's going on. But when you get into the conversation, these feelings and beliefs are still present in the undercurrent, because they are part of you. There is no way to keep them out, and they will thus influence your tone of voice, your wording, your presence, and your reaction to what your partner is saying. There are two ways this can go:

1. You will "coldly" talk about the facts. This will probably not lead to a satisfactory conclusion, because you are discussing something at the level of content and maybe procedure, while the actual problem is playing itself out on the level of emotion and maybe interaction.

2. Or—and this can easily happen in the second stage of the conversation—your fear of losing them will overtake you, and you

will start crying, yelling, or fighting to "prove your point," which, needless to say, will probably not have the desired effect.

The semidetached way of bringing in your real feelings and deep-seated beliefs starts with knowing they are there and accepting that fact, and then talking about them in a compassionate way. You could, for example, say something like "I am so scared that you are no longer in love with me, and I fear losing you" before bringing in a question to explore what is really going on: "What made you stay out so late every night this week?" for example.

THE STORY I'M MAKING UP

Brené Brown, the queen of making feelings a normal part of our conversations, suggests introducing your feelings and beliefs with the following words: "The story I'm making up." Then complete the statement with anything that's going on for you (for example, "The story I'm making up is that you no longer love me" or "...you want to leave me"). By using these words, you introduce the narrative you have been spinning and immediately accept that this may in fact not be what is really going on. It is also a beautiful way to interconnect, as you appreciate both your own feelings and the other person's side of the story by basically saying: "I am experiencing this, but maybe there is a good reason for your actions."

The Undercurrent

As you may have guessed, the levels within communication and the layers within people meet and mingle in our difficult conversations. Like the water flowing around icebergs and waves washing over them, the levels of communication flow around you and the other person. This leads to an interaction between your own iceberg, the other person's iceberg, and these different levels (the water). This interaction, which is called the "undercurrent of a conversation," happens out of sight, but it isn't out of reach if you are willing to take it on.

The undercurrent is the collection of all relevant, but unspoken, feelings, emotions, beliefs, values, and personality traits from all participants in the conversation, and the interaction between them.

What's in the Undercurrent?

The undercurrent is an additional exchange of information on a deeper level, and most often the participants are not (fully) aware of what's going on there. In the undercurrent, you may find things like:

- How you feel about the other person and how they feel about you.

- How both of you feel about yourselves.

- Your emotional state at the moment of the conversation.

- Your beliefs about everything related to the topic of conversation.

- What the conversation is really about.

- Potential solutions, synchronicities, etc.

Every conversation has an undercurrent, and often the undercurrent itself doesn't create any specific problems. But when you, for example, have a conversation with a person that triggers your deepest beliefs about yourself, the undercurrent will be playing a very relevant part in the conversation. In those difficult conversations, the undercurrent is where the actual problem is and where the potential solution can be found. When you talk about what is truly going on for you, you are much more likely to be able to solve what is wrong.

What's the Value of Uncovering What's in the Undercurrent?

Many people aren't happy when feelings or emotions come up in a conversation. Whether they are your own or the other person's, people tend to see emotions surfacing as unhelpful, unnecessary, unprofessional, and childlike, while in fact they are your way into the undercurrent and into the things that really matter. Emotions are a clue that something inside you or the other person is being touched.

And just like a beach ball that does what it's supposed to do when you aren't trying to push it down, when you allow the emotions to take their actual role as a clue and appreciate them for what they are—valuable information—there doesn't have to be anything tricky about them. They can be nothing more or less than information about what is really relevant in the conversation.

A crucial tool for dealing with challenging conversations in a mindful way is to learn to bring out the relevant information that is present in the undercurrent. People who are skilled in this help conversations move to the level where the really relevant information truly lies. Bringing out information from the undercurrent:

- Changes levels of communication to move the conversation to the level where the actual difficulties are.

- Shares relevant aspects of your own iceberg.

- Names the things you sense are going on with the other person in such a way that is constructive and helpful.

Being comfortable bringing out information from the undercurrent is what makes the difference between discussing what's not really relevant and discussing what really matters. Chapter 6 will cover how to bring information from the undercurrent into the conversation in a constructive way so you can find solutions and avoid being stymied by obstacles or old habits.

The Risk of Getting Into Patterns

Many of us find that our difficult conversations play out in the same frustrating way, time and again. The drama triangle is an eye-opening, yet very simple, model created by transactional analysis psychologist Stephen Karpman that makes it abundantly clear why your conversations with some people (often the most important people in your life) so easily spin out of control and into conflict.

Karpman described the model while mapping drama-intense relationships in the late 1960s. The basic idea is that people get easily sucked into playing one of three typical communication "roles." The problem is that these roles and their subsequent interactions are basically a form of pointless role-playing that sucks people into an almost scripted interaction and thus draws parties away from a conscious, mature way of interacting.

What Is the Drama Triangle?

The three roles in the drama triangle are the victim, the rescuer, and the persecutor:

- **The Victim:** the person who feels none of it is their fault, who feels they are at a disadvantage, and who acts as if they do not have any power over the situation.

- **The Rescuer:** the person who, as soon as a victim steps up, offers help or a solution.

- **The Persecutor:** the person who adds their bit to the smoldering situation by pointing the finger and attacking the "victim."

Initially, a drama triangle arises when a person takes on the role of a victim. This person then draws one or more other people into the drama to play one of the other roles of the drama triangle. Often, at least someone will take up the role of rescuer.

The roles are fluid in a way, and therefore various scenarios can occur. For example, the victim might turn on the rescuer, which will motivate the rescuer to switch to the role of persecutor. The reason interactions keep coming back to this pattern is that each participant gets unspoken (and often subconscious) needs or wishes met, without having to acknowledge what is really going on.

The hidden motives of the rescuer are maybe the least obvious, as their helping seems to stem from kindness and generosity. The truth is that they have their own self-interest at heart just as much as the others. Their rescuing is motivated by what they gain from being the person who saves the day. Maybe it's a dependency from the victim, or maybe it's just being known as someone who is supersupportive and helpful, but there is an underlying reason for not allowing the victim to find their own solution—which would help them get out of victimhood instead of keeping them captive in that position.

You, like most people, probably have one preferred role but shift in and out of all of these roles at different points. If you have people with whom conversations seem to fall into the same pattern, no matter what the topic is, the drama triangle might be to blame. We keep falling into old patterns because we allow ourselves to be drawn into these specific roles, which are almost impossible to break free from without self-awareness.

How Can You Break the Cycle?

By becoming more self-aware and understanding the roles you play in your communication with the people around you, you empower yourself, and thus others, to step out of the drama triangle. The Empowerment Dynamic, devised by author David Emerald in 2005, shows the opposite, constructive approach to each of the roles:

- When a victim accepts that they experience vulnerability and have the influence to create another outcome, they shift toward the creator role. They focus on their desired outcome, propelling themselves into action.

- When a persecutor starts building people up while still being positively assertive about their own needs, instead of putting people down through criticizing, blaming, or controlling, they become the challenger, who encourages learning, action, and next steps.

- When a rescuer shows compassion and starts asking questions to help the creator make their plan concrete, they become a coach. A coach provides encouragement and support instead of "rescuing" actions.

It takes only one participant in a conversation to firmly step out of the drama triangle into the empowerment one to open the door for all other participants to go there as well.

Mindful Lesson:
Victim and Persecutor Turn Creator and Challenger

Will and Rebecca have found themselves in one of their recurring conflicts. Will hasn't been feeling happy in his job for a while now. Today, he tells Rebecca about a new example of how his boss doesn't value his work. He's doing so much, above and beyond his job requirements, but still his boss rated him as "average" in his performance review. He feels unseen and underappreciated.

His wife, Rebecca, is irritated. This isn't the first time they have had this discussion. She feels it is time to make a decision: suck it up, have a talk with his boss, or quit and move on. She says, "Will, I have heard you complain about your boss for months now; I really need you to stop that and just do something about it."

Will feels like she's attacking him and is hurt. He watches himself draw further into his shell of victimhood. Then he realizes that by doing that he will take them both deeper into their ineffective fighting style of attacking and defending. He decides to make a different move this time. He says, "I just feel so underappreciated by this review. It is hurtful and diminishes my motivation, as I feel I have worked so hard the past six months. But I also know that complaining to you won't help me feel better. I need to think of how to deal with this. Can you help me brainstorm ideas?"

Rebecca is pleasantly surprised by this change in Will's demeanor. "Of course I can," she says. "I think there are basically three options you can pursue," and she explains the three options. Will considers them and decides he's not ready to quit. Sucking it up hasn't worked so far, so he opts for having a conversation with his boss. They continue to discuss how to set up the conversation to try to make it as effective as possible.

Beyond the Words: Why All These Layers Matter

Here's an idea that might seem radical: Difficult conversations do not happen because of the things you discuss but because you do not discuss the right things in the right way.

It can be overwhelming to think about just how much is going on below the surface of difficult conversations—such as underlying feelings or beliefs, unspoken needs, and unhelpful role-playing. All of these factors contribute to common issues, like the following:

1. Each party is speaking on a different communication level (for example, one person is speaking only on the content level, while the other person is addressing issues on the level of interaction).

2. Emotions come up but are not addressed in a constructive way.

3. The participants avoid discussing the things that really matter, either because of lack of skill or lack of courage.

4. One or both participants have a mindset issue. Some common ones are believing that they are the only person who is right, blaming the other person for how they feel, and believing it is better to hide than to disclose.

5. Neither participant uses information from the undercurrent to move the conversation further.

6. One or both participants fail to listen in a mindful way.

7. One or both participants fail to speak in a mindful way.

8. One or both participants make wrong assumptions about the other person or the situation without checking them.

This list of examples is definitely not complete, but it does give you an idea of how many factors can have an effect on you and the other person in the conversation. The good news is that we all have the ability to start a conversation that does address the right things in the right way. It requires only two things: courage and skill. In Part 2 of this book, you will start the journey of developing the skills to break through these challenges, either inside yourself or the other person.

CHAPTER SUMMARY

The following are takeaways, action steps, and reminders to help you progress smoothly into mindful conflict resolution.

- Conversations have four layers: content, procedure, interaction, and emotion. Sometimes participants are working from different levels of communication, like when one participant keeps speaking on the level of content, while the other person is speaking about their emotions about the situation.

- The high-level reason why conversations can be, or better said, become, difficult is because the participants steer clear of discussing what really matters. You could say that there is a gap between what is being said and what is being thought or experienced, while most often, the things that are not being said are actually really relevant to the problem. They can even be a big step toward the solution!

- Like icebergs, people hide a lot of relevant information about themselves away from others. Nonetheless, all these feelings, beliefs, values, motives, etc. influence us and our interactions with others. It is extremely powerful to know your own iceberg really well and to be able to share the information there with other people.

- The undercurrent of a conversation is where your iceberg interacts with the other person's iceberg. It is the collection of all relevant but unspoken feelings, emotions, beliefs, values, motives, and personality traits from all participants in the conversation, and the interaction between them.

- People can learn to bring information up from the undercurrent, and when they do, it opens up an entirely different way of handling difficult situations. It frees you from being stuck in "mismatched" discussions while at the same time creates space to talk about the things that will really move along your disagreements or conflicts. Even though it's superpowerful to be able to do this, it's not a superpower: It's a skill that can be learned by anyone.

PART 2

ESSENTIAL SKILLS

In this second part of this book, you will learn the essential skills that, when coupled with the background information you learned in Part 1, will give you a toolkit for handling all sorts of challenging communications with grace. Before we explore what to do to make the conflicts you find yourself in run more smoothly, we'll first dive into how your being has an effect on that as well, and how to influence your way of being so it will help you handle conflicts mindfully.

In Chapters 5 and 6, we will discuss the two most important instruments in your communication toolkit: listening and speaking. You will learn the tools to engage mindfully, with the goal of creating a deeper connection with the other participants in the conversation.

The final chapter of this part will bring together everything you've learned in this part so far and form a golden partnership that clarifies what makes conversations run smoothly. At the end of this part, you will be prepared to enter into all sorts of real-life difficult conversations, which we will further discuss in Part 3 of this book.

CHAPTER 4

HOW TO BE IN A DIFFICULT CONVERSATION: PRESENCE & PREPARATION

> "We must be the change we wish to see in the world."
>
> *(attributed to)*
> *Mahatma Gandhi*

Like most other things, difficult conversations require preparation. In this chapter, we'll discuss how you can mentally prepare for a difficult conversation in such a way that you are equipped to use a mindful approach to resolving the disagreement. Your being influences the outcome of difficult conversations, so you'll learn how you can influence your being to promote mindfulness. But first we'll explore what your way of being, your presence, has to do with the outcomes of the confrontation.

The Being Inside the Doing: Presence

Most of the time, people are very much focused on what they should *do*: what they should do to solve a problem, what they should do to have a better connection with other people, or what they should do to solve conflicts in a mindful way.

However, the quote at the start of this chapter doesn't say "do the change," rather "be the change," because the truth is, a very large part of your impact on others doesn't so much result from the things you do, but is in fact a direct effect of the way you are.

How we are is not something we often consider or talk about with others. We tend to either take our way of being for granted ("This is just who I am") or focus on self-development and try to change things about ourselves over a longer period of time ("I'm working on being less selfish"). Yet how we are is also very much related to the present moment and is something we can influence right here and now.

PRACTICE BEING PRESENT ANYTIME

It's so easy to forget that literally every moment offers you the potential to practice your presence and mindfulness skills. While reading this book, you could practice mindfulness by checking in with yourself every few pages: "Am I really here? Am I fully present?" Being able to be fully present, right here, right now, is the base of any mindful approach, so try to practice it in small chunks throughout your day.

What Is Presence?

Your being is closely related to energy. Your body always sends out and absorbs energy, and people pick up on your energy when you enter a room. The best word for this is "presence." Presence, in the way we'll use it here, has two elements to it:

1. Being fully present in the moment.
2. The way you carry yourself, or your bearing. Ideally, you want to aim for natural, authentic self-assurance that creates rapport with others, or in other words, an ability to connect with others.

For the way we use "presence" in this book, the combination of these two elements is crucial.

What Is the Impact of Your Presence?

Personal presence may be one of the most overlooked skills of highly effective people and impactful leaders. It could be overlooked because it's not easy to explain or improve. Some even believe it to be something you are born either with or without. But I believe that presence is something you can develop and grow.

Your personal presence—the energy you bring into a room combined with the level to which you can be in the here and now—reflects in the quality of the relationships that you build and in the levels of safety and trust that people feel when they are with you. This connection (or lack thereof) has to do with the fact that someone has a stronger presence when they have less to hide. If you are considering your own agenda or you are trying to hide certain things (anything from information to your true emotions), two things happen:

1. You cannot be fully present in the moment (because you are also busy hiding stuff).
2. Your energy gets a little distorted from your dishonesty, which impacts your presence.

To understand the second point, it's important to realize that energy is present in every interaction you have. As soon as something is in your mind, you project it out, whether you literally say it or not. People are aware of what's going on inside of you, even though most of the time, they won't be conscious of what it is they are sensing. But it will leave them with the feeling that you are not completely engaged or maybe even that you are not completely honest.

Take, for example, the recognizable situation of not wanting to disappoint someone. Let's say your mother has a new hairdo, which she clearly loves. You really don't like it that much, but you don't want to disappoint her. Instead, you state that you love it. Maybe you say it a little overenthusiastically or maybe you sound a little flat, but unfortunately your mom is likely to sense that you don't in fact like it that much.

A high-level alignment between your inner world and its outer expression builds a strong presence. Presence has internal and external elements to it.

- **Internally**, presence indicates that you are connected to, aware of, and in control of your own inner world, including your authentic emotions, as well as any self-limiting beliefs and negative thoughts you carry with you. (These are often found in the little voice inside that doubts or criticizes you.) You are connected to your mind and your body at the same time, which means you're thinking and feeling at the same time. You're open to and present in the moment.

- **Externally**, presence is how your being influences the people around you. A strong presence leads to a way of interacting that is characterized by real listening and consciously responding, instead of automatically emotionally reacting to the other person.

The more openness and alignment you feel between what's going on inside and what you say and do, the stronger your presence becomes and the more trust you build with yourself and others.

How to Grow Your Presence

Developing and learning to consciously use your personal presence is a big asset when it comes to mindfully handling any type of conversation. Presence is something you always have with you—but it is important to tend to it regularly so it stays strong when situations get challenging.

Strengthening your presence isn't always an easy task, but breaking it down into these four steps can help you focus your efforts effectively.

1. Be Mindful

Presence can exist only when you are consciously connected to what is going on in the here and now—in essence, when you're mindful. Mindfulness makes it possible for you to sense what is going on around you and inside you, so you can more easily tap into the undercurrent and work with it. Making a habit of checking in with yourself frequently throughout the day will help you make mindfulness a lifestyle.

2. Focus on Congruence

Being congruent, meaning there's correspondence between your inner and outer worlds, is something people can sense, even when they aren't consciously aware of it. Recognizing how it feels when you are fully congruent and being able to call it forth is what I believe to be the way into presence. Congruence feels like inner alignment, a sense of being centered in yourself. You could recognize it also as a feeling of being in the flow. Regular (daily) practice of the centering and grounding exercise later in this chapter will support you in building a stronger connection to the feeling of congruence.

3. Listen to Your Inner Voice

We all have an inner voice—whether you call it a "gut feeling," an "intuitive knowing," or just a "sense that you get." This inner knowing is just as valid as the information you get from your five senses. Learn to recognize and trust these other sources of information. How can you do that? Be mindful and present. The voice of your inner knowing is heard much more clearly when you let the dust of the outside world settle and focus your attention inward.

4. Be Aware of Your Personal Energy

Your energy is a vital part of who you are. Finding ways to connect to your energy—and improve it if need be—can help you maintain strong presence. Many people focus on their energy while they practice yoga, meditate, or simply take a walk (outside is best!).

How to Prepare for a Conversation

Just like so many other complicated tasks you do at work and at home, difficult conversations benefit from good preparation. An important note of caution, though: While it is helpful to think of certain points ahead of time, you don't want to try to prepare the whole conversation down to the last word. After all, you want to keep an open mind and be present to what happens as you talk to the other person. Following are some tips for what you can prepare and what's best left to the conversation itself.

What to Leave for the Moment

Many people consider everything that may happen in a difficult conversation ahead of time—what they could say, what the other person may say, and how they will respond to issues that might come up. Even though that may sound like a thorough approach, trying to avoid any surprises is actually a risky way to enter a difficult conversation.

When you prepare something to the level where you worry about the exact wording and the proper order of things, during the conversation itself, you will be working behind the scenes (meaning: in your mind) to have everything happen as it "should be" happening. You are busy trying to say the exact right thing at the exact right time.

You focus on looking for and then recognizing what you expected to happen so you can use your prepared responses to handle it.

If your mind is that busy, you won't be fully present to actually experience what is going on and to figure out how to best respond. Instead of listening and adapting to what is actually happening, you will be going over your mental notes and your strategy. This will compromise your ability to be present and your ability to tap into the undercurrent and to be mindful in your responses.

Imagine a conversation where you are asking your boss for a raise. You have built a rock-solid case for why you should get one. You are ready for anything and everything she could possibly bring up as an argument against it. Then, after you've stated your request, instead of arguing against the raise, your boss offers you an entirely different position, which wouldn't directly lead to an increase in salary, but would mean more responsibility and growth potential. You, however, hear only that there's no raise involved and focus on the arguments why this is not what you want. Because you are so focused on your prepared argumentation, you aren't in touch with what is actually happening and your feelings about that. Before you know it, this cool opportunity is passing you by.

What to Prepare Ahead of Time

The things you can do to prepare for a difficult conversation are all related to how you will be in the conversation itself.

Set an Intention

First things first: It's really helpful to set a constructive intention before you embark on trying to resolve any conflicts or difficulties. Your intention for the conversation is what you intend to create in it and/or through it. Intentions are very powerful—as the saying goes, "energy flows where attention goes," and that is exactly why intentions matter. What you intend with a conversation is what your attention will focus on during the conversation, making it likely that it's created because more energy moves there.

You can revisit the information in Chapter 1 about setting intentions for a refresher, because it's very important to set the right kind of intention. A helpful general guideline for setting your intention is to let your curiosity take the lead. So for example, you may want to set as your intention that you want to gain a better understanding of the other person's perspective. Or you want to find a mutual agreement on how to move forward. An example of a not-so-positive intention would be to intend to make the other person see your point of view.

WHEN A DIFFICULT CONVERSATION HAPPENS UNEXPECTEDLY

Not every difficult conversation is planned in advance. Sometimes they just happen, and you won't have had the opportunity to prepare. Fear not. As you learned in this chapter, overpreparing for a difficult conversation will most likely do more harm than good. If a difficult conversation comes up out of nowhere, take a few deep breaths to center yourself. If you aren't the one initiating the hard talk, know that even though you may not be in the position to postpone the conversation, it is always possible to take a bathroom break to gather your thoughts and to center and ground yourself before engaging. Set your intention on finding a way forward that works and for the words that need to be said to be readily available to you.

Embrace Surprises

Another thing you can do ahead of time is help yourself get comfortable expecting the unexpected and embracing surprises. This is different than trying to imagine every possible scenario, which, as we've discussed, is counterproductive to a mindful discussion. What you want to do instead is practice the mindfulness tenets of acceptance and letting go, along with beginner's mind (discussed in Chapter 1). Yes, things will come up that may scare you, irritate you, or make you angry or sad. By accepting this fact beforehand, you will not be as surprised, so you can approach the situation calmly and by checking in with your energy and feelings instead of reacting emotionally.

Let Go and Trust Yourself

A shift in mindset that can help you prepare for a difficult conversation is to trust that everything you know and feel about the subject will be available to you during the conversation. Sure, you can read through your notes or gather your thoughts beforehand—but once you've done that, *let it go.*

Give your mind permission to just be present in the here and now so it can respond to what is happening. This mindset requires a leap of faith, so begin by experimenting with it in conversations that don't feel too important to you. That way, you'll grow your confidence safely.

Being completely present in the moment will minimize the number of times you experience that feeling after a discussion when you think, "I forgot about X or Y!" or "I should have said X or Y!" By being in the now, the important stuff comes up as it's needed. These afterthoughts should be looked at with care anyway, as they are most often things that come from a win-lose idea of "making them understand." However, it may happen that you realize there is something that you really should have said or done to help create a better outcome. If that is the case, there is no harm in initiating a follow-up conversation.

Center and Ground Yourself

An important physical part of your prep is to center and ground yourself.

- **Centering** means to energetically connect to your inner self.
- **Grounding** means to energetically connect yourself to the earth.

There are many ways to center and ground yourself. Ideally, you would center and ground yourself in a daily meditation practice the morning of your conversation. If you do that, it will take only a couple of deep breaths to come back to a centered and grounded state when walking into that difficult conversation later in the day.

If those breaths are not enough and/or you feel a little anxious and disconnected, try the following quick little practice. This will take you only about five minutes, and you can even do it in the restroom before you walk into your meeting.

AN EASY CENTERING AND GROUNDING PRACTICE

This easy and fast practice is inspired by a guided meditation from Alan Seale. It works wonderfully well to ground and center yourself.

Sit comfortably. It's helpful to close your eyes, to minimize distraction and keep your focus on your own energy. Become aware of your body, just sitting. Feel the clothes on your body. Feel the air flowing past your skin. Listen to the sounds around you, close by and farther away. Shift your awareness to your breath, at first just by noticing where your breath is right now. Then, invite your breath to go all the way into your belly. Breathe in and out as if breathing through your belly button. Notice the effect on your body and on your mind.

Then, bring your attention to your tailbone. Imagine a grounding cord going down from your tailbone into the earth. Whatever form it takes is perfectly fine. Imagine, visualize, or feel this energetic cord going deeper and deeper into the earth, past the layers of soil, and rock, and minerals, until it reaches the center of the earth. Imagine it fastening itself there. And then, imagine that through this cord you can breathe up grounding and stabilizing earth energy. Imagine it having a color. Feel that energy enter your body at the tailbone, flowing all the way through your body, energizing all of your cells on its path. Continue to breathe in slowly and deeply, exhaling completely.

When you've followed that earth energy all the way up, allow it to flow through your crown, into the sky above your head. Then imagine that from the farthest reaches of the universe, the central star, there's a beam of light coming your way. Imagine it having a color too. Imagine this light, which is inspirational and creative in nature, flowing in through your crown and then flowing down through your head, neck, chest, and stomach and down through your legs, out through your feet. Continue to breathe that earth energy and that light from the sky through your body. After a few breaths like this, slowly bring yourself back to the here and now, feeling your body again, breathing deeply to reawaken your body. When you feel ready, open your eyes.

Centering and grounding also makes it easier for you to be able to accept the other person's standpoint, even when they are not agreeing with you. That's because the need to be confirmed in your perspective is less strong when you are deeply connected to your own truth. Centering and grounding will do that.

Check In with Your Mood and Energy

Another useful way to prepare yourself ahead of time is to get yourself in the right "vibe." This includes your energy level, but also your general mood.

The energy you project outward, knowingly or unknowingly, will influence the impact you make on the other person. By making sure your energy vibrates with optimism, lightheartedness, sincerity, a sense of humor, and compassion, you will influence the interaction accordingly.

Your energy is something you can easily influence by moving your body. So even if your day didn't start out great and you're not feeling energetic, you can shift your energy toward lightheartedness and openness through movement. Movement activates stagnant energy and shifts how you feel in the present moment.

SHAKE IT OUT

Shifting your energy is really simple: Begin by shaking your hands and your arms. Next, shake your legs and your hips. Move your head from side to side. Move your shoulders up and down. Then do an allover body shake. Redo this whole procedure a couple of times. Move and shake for at least a minute, maybe even two. Put on some high-energy music to help!

When you're done, stand completely still and notice the effect the shaking has had on your body, your energy, and your state of mind.

One of the fastest and most effective ways to do this is to shake your body (see sidebar). Other quick and fun ways to change your energy are dancing and running. You'll become instantly more aware of your energy and how it affects your mood and your way of interacting with others. And when you are more aware, you can take more ownership of it and change it if need be.

Taking "ownership" of your energy means that you take full responsibility for the energy you send out into the world. After becoming aware of how easy it is to change your energy, it's no longer appropriate to hold on to the belief that your energy is just happening to you. You control it.

How to Prepare Your Mindset

The mental attitude with which you enter an argument or difficult conversation will help determine your responses to and your interpretations of the other person's words and behavior. Your mindset is thus a very powerful tool to influence your being and your subsequent behavior in difficult conversations. You can affect your mindset by considering the following factors.

Think Win-Win, Not Win-Lose

As discussed in Chapter 1, when choosing a mindful approach to handling difficult conversations, success takes on a different meaning. This is also related to the topic of interconnection and the And Stance as discussed in Chapter 2. In essence, you want to remember that your partner has their own perspective on what makes you two disagree. Explore that! Search for their reason and their story, and open up to finding a way forward that embraces both your perspectives. That's how you let go of a win-lose mentality ("If you win, I must lose") and replace it with a win-win mentality.

Maintain an Open (Not Armored) and Vulnerable Attitude

Staying open is closely related to the topic of vulnerability. Since Brené Brown's groundbreaking books and her epic TED Talk titled "The Power of Vulnerability" (see the Online Resources section at the back of this book), this hard-to-discuss but very relevant topic is front of mind for many people, even in the workplace.

Being vulnerable means taking the risk of emotional exposure. Vulnerability is not necessarily good or bad, but "to feel is to be vulnerable," says Brown. So the truth is, as people, we just are vulnerable, so there's not much we can do about that. Of course, we often try not to be vulnerable nonetheless, and that leads to wearing armor to prevent ourselves from being hurt and our feelings from being seen.

In difficult conversations, that's a big challenge. How can you be open and connected when you are hiding within a suit of armor?

Allow Emotions to Surface

To be able to be mindful in solving conflicts, you must allow the feelings residing in your iceberg to come to the surface and become part of your experience. Your feelings in any given moment offer you a treasure trove of information about what is going on with you, and even with the other person. This emotional insight will help you uncover information from the undercurrent and help you discuss what is really going on. So in fact, wanting to be able to handle difficult conversations mindfully invites you to accept your own vulnerability and use it to propel you toward solutions. Your vulnerability is not something to be afraid of; it's something to invite in and learn from. It also offers a way for other people to really connect with you.

This mindset is quite different from what people are used to doing, though. The truth is that dealing with powerful emotions (or any emotions, for that matter) is not something most of us have much experience with. At school and work, we're usually taught (either explicitly or implicitly) that emotions should be quickly hushed, acknowledged briefly (if at all), then stored away. All in all, we have very little to no experience being around or handling strong emotions.

This inexperience and subsequent discomfort with emotions is highly self-reinforcing: Every emotion that comes up is quickly "corrected" by our peers or family members, thus allowing little space to experience the actual emotion, which in turn reinforces a low comfort level around emotions.

Objectively speaking, emotional outbursts are simply what happens when unexpressed feelings in your iceberg rise to the surface. Especially in the workplace, but surprisingly in many other situations, too, people do not express in a timely manner what they feel, sense, or truly experience. By not speaking their truth, people bottle up all the feelings they do not express, piling one on top of the other, which allows their emotions to inflate like a balloon. And we all know what happens when we keep blowing air into a balloon: At some point it will burst. When this happens and an emotional outburst occurs, it often feels like an overreaction to the situation at hand.

Mindful Lesson: Emotional Leakage

Alice has been coming in late for meetings all day because her calendar is completely overbooked. She has just had a conversation with her boss, Martin. He told her that he won't be approving the proposal she prepared because he thinks it's not good enough.

Alice had worked really hard on that proposal, and hearing Martin's assessment of it made her feel sad and underappreciated. It also made her question her own skills, as she often does already anyway. She didn't say anything about any of this to Martin, though, because she didn't want him to think she was defensive or taking things too personally.

After her meeting with Martin, Alice literally runs down the corridor because she is late for her meeting with Ben. Ben greets her by saying, "It's good of you to show up, finally..." Alice bursts into tears, and yells at him: "That's so uncalled for. I have been trying so hard!"

What happened to Alice is what we call "emotional leakage." Emotional leakage happens when a person's inner feelings are revealed and expressed more intensely than would seem appropriate for the situation, or to a different person altogether, because they are largely related to something in the past. In this case, Alice was already under pressure from running around all day.

Her meeting with Martin brought up some strong feelings and negative beliefs about herself, which she didn't appropriately share with Martin but instead bottled up. When coming into her meeting with Ben with this buildup of emotions and stress, one small but unkind remark was enough to make her explode.

Work with Emotions

What happens when we feel our emotions would be completely different if we treated feelings as a source of valuable information from the start. If feelings are treated as a normal part of the conversation, they are something you can just talk about. For example, you could say something like "I notice this hurts me" or "I feel sad hearing you say that." If you use your feelings as information, and make them part of the conversation, they won't have a chance to build up and cause an outburst of strong emotions at a later time.

Dealing with emotions that surface in a difficult conversation starts with awareness and a calm attitude. There's no need to be scared of emotions or to be afraid that the conversation will spin out of control.

Take one or two seconds to find clarity and put yourself on the right track to handle the emotions (yours or the other person's) in an effective way. In those seconds, you will be able to recognize that there is an emotion present. That's enough. After that, you can take a step back and evaluate which emotion it is. When you know, you can name it—to yourself, if it's yours, or out loud if it's the other person's ("I see you're angry," for example). When the emotion is "called out," it will deflate.

This simple five-step plan will allow you to mindfully handle emotions:

1. Recognize there is an emotion present.

2. Take a step back to consider it.

3. Name the emotion.

4. Watch or experience the emotion (and maybe see a new emotion coming up).

5. Talk about the emotion and the underlying feelings, or work with the new emotion.

It's a powerful practice to really get to know your feelings. If you make yourself have an honest look at the feelings you are having, you will explore your inner world in a way that will pay off when you are in a difficult situation. It takes practice to recognize your feelings, but if you consciously invite your feelings to just be there, without judgment or trying to push them away, you will gain experience in being around them. And the more experience you have with your feelings, the less they will scare you when they surface in a difficult conversation or conflict.

Don't Judge Feelings

There are dozens of different feelings, all with slightly different connotations. It's also relevant to acknowledge that experiences can be labeled as negative: for example, the feeling "stressed." As part of your mindfulness practice, try to reserve judgment on feelings. You can even start to see other "sides" of feelings with negative connotations. For example, see if you can observe the same "stressed" experience in a more neutral way, like "busy," or even in a positive way, like "recognized" or "sought after." The way you choose to approach your emotions can shift your entire experience of them.

TRY JOURNALING

If talking about your emotions feels difficult at first, a really helpful method is to write about your experiences, the feelings those experiences bring forth, and the thoughts you have about those feelings. This process will help you realize that feelings themselves don't make you unhappy; it's, in fact, the thoughts you have about them that will. Choose a time and place to be by yourself. You may want to use a guided meditation to get still and connect to your feelings. You can also just explore inside yourself what feelings are present with you. Try to notice the feelings without sinking into them, and start freewriting about what comes up for you.

CHAPTER SUMMARY

The following are takeaways, action steps, and reminders to help you progress smoothly into mindful conflict resolution.

● The way we are in a difficult conversation is an often overlooked element that you can have total control over. You can take full ownership of your energy, your presence, and thus how you influence the energy in the room. The energy you project may actually have a bigger impact on the other person than what you say.

● Developing your personal presence and learning to consciously use it is a big asset. You can start developing your presence by consciously being more present in the moment, strengthening your connection to your energy, and listening to your inner voice.

● People tend to prepare their difficult conversations in way too much detail. This will lead you to be stuck in your head, while you should be present to pick up on what's really needed in the moment.

● You shouldn't prepare the exact wording, the proper order of things, or detailed ideas about the specific result you are trying to reach. You should prepare your intention, your mindset (for example, to expect the unexpected or to trust that the right solution will emerge), and your way of being (for example, by centering and grounding yourself).

● Managing emotions isn't as hard as people often fear. Recognizing the emotion, naming it, and just being okay with the fact that it's there (whether it's your own or the other person's) is how you can allow emotions to flow through the conversation without hijacking it.

CHAPTER 5
HOW TO LISTEN MINDFULLY

"Most people do not listen with the intent to understand; they listen with the intent to reply."

Stephen R. Covey

Listening is widely considered to be the most important communication skill. Some research says that we listen during approximately 45 percent of the time spent in communication, while the rest is divided between speaking, writing, and reading. Interestingly, however, people spend much more time "officially" learning to speak, read, or write than they do learning to listen. This is true for our school system, and for adult learning as well; a quick online search for courses on improving communication skills offers three to five times more hits for speaking or writing than for listening. It's easy to see how listening is an underrated and underdeveloped skill. Yet it's especially important in mindfulness practice to have a solid understanding of how to listen with an open mind, compassion, and generosity.

The Problem with Shallow Listening

Imagine this: You're in the middle of an intense conversation, and the other person is speaking. You are quiet and allowing the other person to speak their mind. While you're listening, thoughts run through your head, like "This point they're making is absolutely invalid; how can I prove that?" or "This approach really doesn't help my situation, and I will explain why as soon as they stop talking."

When the other person is done speaking, you embrace your turn to talk. You either begin by explaining why everything they have said is absolutely invalid/irrelevant/untrue/etc., or you simply set their input aside and share your own perspective on the situation.

Sound familiar? It probably does! This, of course, is not mindful listening, and it won't help you get through difficult conversations or conflicts. This common scenario happens because our brains are capable of processing information much more quickly than people can speak. This is part of the reason why we find ourselves so easily distracted when we should be paying attention. While the other person is explaining their point of view, your brain is looking for something to do. We are just so used to focusing on ourselves that, out of habit and for efficiency's sake, our brains switch to structuring our own thoughts. But there is a much more interesting and more effective way to use your brainpower: deeper listening.

The Benefits of Deeper Listening

It's easy to say that you should improve your listening to be able to solve conflicts in a mindful way, but do you really know what the benefits of better listening can be? Let's take some time to explore the many reasons why listening on a deeper level will enhance your conflict resolution skills.

Listening Fosters a Cooperative Environment

First things first: Listening in a mindful way creates an atmosphere of cooperation and openness. Really being present with the other person and using all your senses to understand their perspective shows them respect, and, no surprises here—people love that. People love to be listened to, heard, and valued. It can affect them deeply, and because you helped shape that atmosphere, they will open up a deeper connection with you. That, in turn, leads to more trust and thus to a more open dialogue.

Inviting More Sharing

The second big advantage is that by listening mindfully, you encourage the person to move to the emotional level of communication. People usually love to speak about themselves; by allowing someone to do that without interruption or immediate responses, they are more likely to get into details about their motivations and beliefs. Those details allow you to get a better understanding of why they behave the way they do and thus why you are having this difficult conversation with them in the first place. It may also give you information about what they need to be able to resolve the conflict.

Mindful Lesson:
Insights Through Deeper Listening

Arla and Emily have been really good friends since college. They still meet every month to catch up. Today, they are out for brunch. They have been going over both of their private lives in the past hour or so, and now Arla is talking about some recent experiences at her job. Her manager has been quite absent, which has given Arla the feeling of being without guidance in a job that is still relatively new to her. She feels highly uncertain because of that, taking away part of the joy that she initially felt for the job. It's a pretty long story, and Arla is starting to feel a little guilty for taking up so much space in their limited time together.

Emily isn't complaining, though—on the contrary, she seems to be fully invested in listening to everything Arla has to say. She is looking at Arla, nodding now and then, but is not making any move that indicates her wanting to jump in, cut the story short, or share her own experience in something similar. Her calm presence is inviting Arla to continue and helps her go even deeper into the situation and her feelings about it.

Now that she can finish her train of thought fully (something she hasn't been able to do since the trouble with her manager started), Arla realizes that her insecurity isn't something brought on by her manager. The fact that her manager allows her so much space is in fact a very positive sign, which should make her feel more confident, not less.

The insight surprises her, but she feels it's true. Her manager is not trying to make her insecure; she is actually empowering her. Then and there, Arla experiences a shift in perspective and decides to start behaving accordingly come Monday morning. She hugs her friend, thanking her for listening and for being so fully present with her.

A Warning

The reasons to listen mindfully boil down to this fact: If you listen better, the other person will share more information with you. While this strategy is truly compassionate and cooperative and can lead you to better conflict outcomes, it could also be manipulated into a communication "trick" if you pretend to be a mindful listener. Tricking someone in this way is useless, though, because mindful listening is inherently done with sincerity. Mindful listening originates in seeing the value of connecting and understanding and thus finding solutions to difficult conversations or conflicts. If you simply murmur and nod while zoning out, people will sense intuitively that your interest is insincere.

How to Listen Mindfully

Like with any other skill, you'll have to practice listening mindfully to become proficient at it. You'll see many of the same themes you've been learning about—layers of communication, undercurrents, tenets of mindfulness—come up again in this section.

Listen at the Right Level(s)

You can listen to information you hear during a difficult conversation at several levels. The straightforward model used here works well to explain those various levels. You could be listening in order to:

1. Reply

2. Gain clarity

3. Connect

4. Find the way forward

Listening to Reply

The first type of listening is all about you and your monkey mind (see Chapter 2). Instead of bringing your attention to the other person, you stay inside your own mind and basically start a second (internal) discussion alongside the one you are already having.

This internal discussion is what is called "inner chatter" of your monkey mind. You are wondering how to judge the other person's contribution: "Are they right, or are they wrong? How smart is their contribution? Do I believe what they are saying?" You may also consider what you feel about the other person: "Do I like them? Are they nice? What do I think of how they present themselves?" Also, you are considering your possible response. Essentially, you are being quiet until it is your time to speak.

Listening to Gain Clarity

Listening to gain clarity, the second level of listening, is where you shift from listening to your own ideas to listening to the other person. This listening is very factual, though. The acting participant on this level, just like it was on the first level, is "thought," or the intellectual brain. The intellectual brain is great at tasks like analyzing, structuring information, and making plans.

In listening to the other person speak, the intellectual brain will be trying to distinguish between things that prove and things that disprove what it already knows, things that fit and things that don't fit into its analysis of the world so far. It's trying to understand the other person on an intellectual level. There is learning, but there is also judgment, just like on the first level, and it's clear that the first and second levels can easily be combined.

Listening to Connect

On the third level of listening, a big shift happens as we move from the intellectual, thinking mind to the intuitive, feeling mind. The intention in this type of listening is to really connect with the other person and understand them on an emotional level. Needless to say, this level of listening is definitely not purely an intellectual process, like the first two are.

That said, the first step of understanding someone is an intellectual one. You have to cognitively grasp what they are saying to even come close to understanding them. But it definitely doesn't stop there. The type of listening at this stage is empathic in nature, meaning you try to hear not only what people literally say but also what they mean and feel underneath that. Understanding them on that deeper level builds a true connection with them. To be able to do that, you'll have to put yourself in the other person's shoes and try to get the full picture of what things are like for them.

When we move to this level of listening, we engage our intuitive, emotional mind and try to make sense of how the other person is feeling. In listening to connect, you refrain from inserting your opinions or thoughts. You leave your judgment at home.

There is no way to listen empathically, to really connect to someone, when you are also judging them, be it moral ("This is right" or "This is wrong"), on a cognitive level ("This is different from what I know"), or by assuming you know how they will finish their sentence (and even finishing it for them). This third level of listening is really not about you; it's about the other person.

To be able to hear people on this level, you listen to the words they are saying, but you don't stop there. By applying meaning to the choice of words and the images these words convey, you learn so much more about what they believe. Words and images don't come up out of nothing. Even if the other person didn't choose them consciously, subconsciously, they did. And that is relevant.

You probably guessed that to understand people on an emotional level, you also need to listen to their emotions. And that isn't as hard as it sounds. Emotions flow into the conversation through our voices: the tone, but also the pace, silences, and other vocal variety, like if you hear someone's voice break or they struggle with a tightness in their throat. All of these elements are relevant, since they give you information about the emotions the other person is experiencing while saying the things they say. All of this data gives you a lot to work with as you connect and try to move forward.

Mindful Lesson:
Listening to Emotions

Brothers Michael and Frank get along really well most of time. Even though they don't live in the same city, they speak over the phone almost weekly, so they are well informed about each other's lives. Lately, Frank has been struggling a little. His job is extremely demanding and his family life is busy and intense too. His wife has a big deadline coming up, and this week, his son started school for the first time. All of these factors are definitely adding to his feelings of stress.

When Michael asks Frank about planning their mutual trip to their hometown to spend time with their parents, Frank responds agitatedly. He starts explaining the challenges he is facing in managing his work and maintaining at least a sense of balance between that and his private life. He has had no time to look up flights, and he doesn't expect that will change soon. Come to think of it, he doesn't know if he will have time to fly out at all in the coming months.

Michael knows Frank was really looking forward to spending time with their parents, so Frank's words surprise him. While listening to Frank, Michael takes a metaphorical step back to consider what is going on. He listens beyond the actual words and notices how Frank's tone of voice shifts from calm to agitated. He takes this as a clue as to what might be going on: Frank may want to spend time with his family, but he feels so overwhelmed with the pressure of work and everything that is going on at home that it's all too much for him, which causes him to lash out. Michael allows Frank to complete his full story. He then says, "It's clear you are extremely busy at the moment, but I get the impression that you would like to go see Mom and Dad if you didn't have to organize it yourself. Is that right?"

Frank hesitates, then confirms this is the case. "That's true—I would like to take a break and go see them, but I just don't know where to find the time to look for flights and make it happen."

"But it's not much trouble for me to find you a flight too, man!" says Michael. "What would be a good weekend to go?" And they discuss when would be the least intrusive weekend to go. Frank feels heard and valued, and Michael is happy they still get to go together.

Listening to Find the Way Forward

Lastly, we come to the level of listening that is the most difficult to explain, the hardest to learn, and the most rewarding of them all. This is where the intuitive mind is really going all out, as it is working to find a way forward that will overcome the challenges in the conversation and solve the conflict. This type of listening opens both parties in the conversation up to possibilities that none of them had in mind before.

On this level of listening you tap into the undercurrent. We'll talk more about this later in this chapter.

Listening Using Mindful Tenets

The big challenge in listening mindfully during a difficult conversation is twofold:

1. You'll have to stay fully present in the situation to be able to pick up on everything that is going on and the potential that is arising.

2. You'll have to refrain from habitually reacting (internally or out loud) to what you hear and to the emotional reaction you experience as a result.

Bringing a mindful attitude into a difficult conversation is a powerful way to help with both. Let's have a look at some of the mindful habits that will support your listening, and how to cultivate them in difficult conversations.

Set an Intention

If you know beforehand that you will be having a difficult conversation, prepare yourself by setting a helpful, supportive intention (see Chapter 1). Your intention could be, for example, "to find a way out of the conflict that respects both parties" or "to gain mutual understanding."

Your listening and your presence will be charged with that intention, allowing the intention to infuse the general "energy" in the room.

Be Present at the Beginning

Being present is of crucial importance to being able to listen well. When coming into a potentially difficult conversation, allow yourself time to arrive and slow down to really take it in: Where are you exactly, who is there, how do you feel in this setting, etc.?

Following this next procedure will quickly bring you into your body and make you present in the here and now.

- (Re)connect to your body as soon as you sit down. This will help you be and stay present with everything that may come up.

- Place both feet on the ground.

- Breathe into your abdomen, bringing you into your body and thus helping you be present with the experience.

If a conversation unexpectedly turns into conflict, you may not have "prepared" yourself, but it won't be too late to breathe and bring in a mindful approach.

Use All Your Senses to Listen

This mindfulness aspect is especially important to listening. Apart from your hearing, it's helpful to consciously bring in your other senses to gather information about what's really going on. Sight may be the obvious one, since you'll likely watch the other person's body language, but remember that we do not speak about your "gut feeling" or something "leaving a bitter taste" for nothing. Practice sensing the whole experience and picking up information beyond mere words.

Stay Fully Present for the Duration

After the initial focus on becoming present, work on staying present with the experience, however hard that may be. Many of us check out of conversations to think about the past or the future, taking us away from what is really happening in the moment, especially when what is happening in the moment isn't something we are happy about, like when we are on the receiving end of constructive—

or not-so-constructive—feedback. The practice here is to consistently be present with and aware of the experience as it takes place and to accept things as they are right now.

Pause

You could say that listening is one big opportunity to pause, observe, and experience. But, in your silence, there is the risk of going into inner chatter, a.k.a. your monkey mind, judgment, labeling, etc. Instead, make the conscious decision to pause in order to refocus your mind on the valuable inner experience of emotions and insights, instead of letting it go into a tailspin of negativity, reactivity, and drama.

Keep an Open Mind
(Using Nonjudgment, Curiosity, and Trust)

Judging is not helpful in resolving conflicts. The underlying outcome of judging is to separate instead of to connect. In accepting things as they are, you refrain from judging them and labeling them as good or bad. Instead, choose curiosity to approach information.

Curiosity is, of course, helpful to gain a better understanding of what the other person is saying. It can help you read signals about the energy and atmosphere in the room. It is also a great way to bring conscious awareness to your own emotions and your reactions to what is being said.

Trust is another important aspect of the open mind in listening. Trust in your intuitive mind, trust that a way forward will come up, and trust that, if you let go of judging and thinking about how to respond, the right words will come when it is your turn to speak.

Remembering all of these mindfulness practices will make you a more thoughtful, compassionate, and involved listener. Practice them like any other skill when you get small chances in everyday life—that way, they are easier to call to mind when you're in a difficult conversation.

Listening to Yourself

After all the information you've learned thus far in this chapter, you might believe that listening to the other person is the beginning and end of great listening. But the truth is, it isn't. You also need to listen to someone else, namely *you*. Yes, listening to yourself is also a component of mindful listening.

Of course, this does not refer to your monkey mind's inner chatter, but to the emotions, beliefs, and needs that come up in your interaction with the other person; your intuition; and your gut feeling. All of these give you hints on how to move forward.

While listening to the other person's words, and understanding them on a deep level, emotions and ideas surface for you too. You could say that their words trigger emotions somewhere in your iceberg. They touch emotions, beliefs, or values, and you automatically experience a response to that. That response, naturally, can be positive, but in a difficult conversation, it is more likely to be something like discomfort, anger, resentment, or fear.

If you encouraged these naturally occurring reactions to stay on a subconscious level, and just started to speak in response to the other person's words, there's a big chance that your subconscious reactions would still trickle into the conversation (or come in with a parade!). This situation would probably not lead to a more constructive conversation, because important emotions aren't being shared and addressed.

Listening to Yourself Provides Lots of Information

One way to prevent that type of emotional leakage is to listen to yourself and notice what is happening inside you. The challenge here is to become consciously aware of what is being triggered and take ownership of it. This basically means accepting it as information without judgment. That way, your emotions aren't leading you on a spin of reactive behavior—instead, you are owning your emotions by speaking about them when it is your turn to speak.

Also, in hearing the other person speak, your intuitive mind, or gut feeling, is probably giving you hints on how to proceed. Ideas come up that may not have been anywhere in your conscious mind before the conversation. As with the emotions, it is your challenge to bring these into your conscious awareness and use them to resolve the conflict or disagreement.

This is where that extra brainpower you've freed up by listening without monkey mind chatter or judgment comes in handy. Use that brainpower to explore and come to terms with what happens inside you when you listen to the other person speak. Grab hold of those floating thoughts and ideas that may suddenly come up.

How to Listen to Constructive Criticism

One of the most difficult challenges in listening arises when you are on the receiving end of constructive, or not-so-constructive, criticism or feedback. However mindfully you are trying to approach things, it's not easy to hear about the other person's problems with you. But feedback is one important way to learn about your weaknesses and the impact you make on others. Without constructive criticism, you won't improve. It may not be fun, but it is important.

Feedback isn't easy to receive, but it's also not easy to give. Because constructive criticism is so often met with hostility and defensiveness, many people refrain from giving feedback altogether. You could meet the ones who do go out of their way to tell you how you could improve with at least appreciation for their courage. Beyond that, when trying to learn what there is to learn from any criticism you receive, there are a few things to consider.

Removing the Shields

Often when you realize someone is going to tell you something you can improve on, your automatic response will be to close off, to shield yourself, especially your heart, from hurt and attack. This is a logical response that you may have adopted after years of dealing with emotional "attacks" growing up.

These attacks may have been on the large or small side, depending on your personal situation, but almost all children have a tough time dealing with people telling them what they think of them (often without any mindful attitudes being present). Remember the playground spats, the comments about your body in gym class, or being punished for something your sibling or classmate did? Without the skills to handle them, even these "normal" attacks were painful. Most kids deal with these common scenarios by learning to protect, or shield, themselves from being hurt by comments like that. However helpful it seems to be at that time, shielding has a big downside: It not only protects you from the bad, but it also closes out the good. Things like love, appreciation, and validation cannot enter through the shield either. So in avoiding the bad, you prevent yourself from having the good too.

Shielding is understandable for children who lack the grown-up skills to deal with criticism, but as an adult, you ideally learn that you are okay as you are and that other people do not decide how valuable you are. You can also develop the skills to handle criticism better, such as turning it into what it really is: someone's opinion about how you could improve, instead of a big harsh truth.

Even though shielding is no longer necessary as an adult, it's hard to let go of. Many people never stop shielding, unfortunately. But there are two big advantages if you do:

1. You open yourself up to all that good stuff.

2. You open yourself up to a much deeper connection with people, even the ones who may have something "constructive" to say to you.

Those two benefits can help you get through (or avoid) difficult conversations.

Practicing Discernment

Among other things, listening to feedback and accepting that someone has an opinion about you is a lesson in discernment. Sometimes the criticism you receive is helpful; sometimes it's not. You need to decide how to work with it, or not. But first you have to be able to take it in.

After all, criticism is multifaceted:

1. Often there is some sort of fact involved: something that you did or said, for example.

2. Next, there is what this fact says about you, your opinions, your personality, your mindset at the time, etc.

3. Then, there's what this fact triggered in the other person: where it touched something in their iceberg. It's important to appreciate that the feedback you get says as much about them as it does about you.

THE OTHER WAY AROUND

Of course, the information about accepting criticism is true the other way around as well: If you have feedback for someone else, it's wise to always explore what it says about you, and how their behavior touched you in your values, beliefs, fears, emotions, and so on. Own that, and be courageous about it by sharing what was touched in you when they behaved as they did.

Receiving Criticism with Dignity

Being open to receive feedback is a powerful skill. Allowing people to share how your behavior touched them makes your relationship with them open, and often deeper. It takes only one moment of awareness to get into the right vibe to hear what they want to share with you. Follow these steps to set up an open, compassionate atmosphere:

1. Acknowledge what is going on. Realize that in essence, someone

is simply sharing their opinion with you: nothing more, nothing less. This opinion might be spot-on, but it can also be off the mark. To be able to decide which one it is, you'll have to really understand what they are saying.

2. Open yourself to receive their message. Clear your mind of other things, take a deep breath, let go of defensiveness and shielding, suspend any judgment, and prepare to really listen.

3. Listen to understand, without interrupting. When they are finished, check if you understood correctly ("I understand that I really hurt you when I decided not to go visit Grandma with you; is that correct?").

4. Say thank you. It's not easy to give feedback. Sincerely thank the other person for taking the courage to confront you.

5. Ask questions to deconstruct what is really going on. For example, try to get clear if it is a recurring thing or an isolated incident ("Do you see me blow off family gatherings a lot? Do you feel I am not there for Grandma?"). Also try to determine if this is their opinion alone or if other people feel the same way ("Has Grandma said anything about it to you?"). Ask if there are any concrete solutions they see ("How do you think I could make up with her?").

6. Create time to think about your next steps. At work, how you deal with it may affect your future in the company. At home, your decision about how to respond influences your relationships. On the other hand, your own opinion is really relevant too. This is where discernment is needed What is really going on, and where do you want to go with that? Give yourself some time to consider before responding.

7. Tell them how you will respond to their criticism. After considering (sometimes this may be the same day, sometimes later), you should share your next steps. Maybe you make amends to some-

one, maybe you have to redo part of a project, and maybe your decision will be to do nothing. In any case, be open about your follow-up to their feedback.

Bringing It All Together: Become a Mindful Listener

To listen in such a way that you are connected to both yourself and the other person and that allows you to tap into the undercurrent and find unexpected solutions, you need to be focused on:

- **The other person:** Learn from them, especially about how they see things, and always to connect with them deeply. This requires you to refrain from judging and to instead be curious.

- **Yourself:** Use the opportunity to pause while listening and gather information inside yourself as to how you experience what is being said by the other person. Listen with all your senses while engaging and trusting your intuitive mind to make sense of all the information you pick up in and around you and bring it to a fully conscious level.

If you do all that, then, and only then, are you led into what you could call a field of new opportunities. This is a very promising place to be, as in this field of opportunities, ideas emerge on how to move forward in a way that respects both positions and helps solve the conflict or disagreement. An idea often comes up as a seemingly unrelated thought or a synchronicity (meaningful coincidence). For example, while listening to your colleague explaining the challenges of coming up with a great strategy to launch that product, you hear her share everything she's rejected. Suddenly, an idea pops up in your head that combines some of the elements of her ideas, but without the downsides. When you are open to these opportunities and recognize them for what they are, you can use them in your speaking and thus steer the conversation in a positive direction.

Practice, Practice, Practice

Becoming a really great listener requires awareness and practice. Now that you've read this chapter, you have awareness. So, let's get to the practicing.

Take a look at your calendar right now: What meetings (work or personal) in the coming week could be a good place to start practicing mindful listening? It doesn't have to be a potential conflict or difficult conversation—any meaningful discussion will do. Choose at least one, preferably a couple.

Before you go into these meetings, set a clear intention for yourself. If you've chosen a work meeting, this could be something like "find out everything about X's position on...," and if you're going with a personal meeting, maybe use something like "find out how Y is feeling now that she's been in her new job for over a month."

While you're in the meeting, focus on being present and make an effort to listen from an empathic standpoint. Really try to get where the other person is coming from. Also, be aware when you accidentally switch to one of the "lower" levels of listening.

After you've practiced this at least twice, start adding the other elements you've learned in this chapter, one by one. Use the various aspects of a mindful attitude (not necessarily all at once), then listen to yourself on an empathic level, and then try to connect to the opportunities that your intuitive mind may pick up on. In a nonconflict situation, these will not be solutions, as there isn't a problem, but maybe there will be an invitation to spend more time together or to work on a project as a team.

Developing the skill of mindful listening will certainly take practice, but keep it light: Take some notes afterward to keep track of your progress, share your "results" with friends and/or the people you had the conversations with if appropriate, and always enjoy your wins!

CHAPTER SUMMARY

The following are takeaways, action steps, and reminders to help you progress smoothly into mindful conflict resolution.

- Listening is highly undervalued as a communication skill, yet it is one of the most important skills to develop when you want to embrace a mindful approach to conflict resolution.

- Taking time to really listen to someone is respectful, and it allows the other person to dig deep and uncover everything they think and feel about a certain subject. In mindful listening, curiosity is key. This creates a deeper connection between the two of you, which has a positive effect on finding a way forward that works for both of you.

- It's important to be aware of the fact that you can listen to the other person on different levels, and that these levels offer you different kinds of information about the other person's position.

- Listening to yourself is very important too. It can help you connect with your intuition.

- To listen mindfully, you must stay fully present in the situation so that you may be able to pick up on everything that is going on, while at the same time not reacting immediately to what you hear.

- Feedback isn't necessarily fun or easy to digest, but it is one of the only ways to really understand how you impact others. Instead of shielding yourself when you receive criticism, try to be open and really take in what the other person is trying to tell you. When you fully understand, consider how you want to work with that. It is always your choice how to work with other people's opinions about you.

- Bringing in mindful behavior, like setting a positive intention, pausing, and keeping an open mind, supports the way you listen and helps you access the information in the undercurrent. Through that, you will open up to recognize the (unexpected) potential solutions that emerge.

CHAPTER 6
HOW TO SPEAK MINDFULLY

"Let your tongue speak what your heart thinks."

Davy Crockett

In this chapter, you will learn how to best share your truth as you discuss a difficult topic. Remember, one of the primary reasons to have a difficult conversation is to share your feelings on a topic, so mindful speaking is truly as important as mindful listening. If you don't speak up, people won't know what you think, feel, or believe, which can be highly frustrating and lead to less trust and connection. You'll also learn how to look beyond the main topic so that you can see what other factors might be playing into your conversation and how you should talk about them.

Finding the Right Balance

We've all dealt with a huge range of speaking styles. Babies who can't speak yet will try to make you understand how they feel or what they want and need from you, but as their repertoire is limited to crying, and later various forms of sign language, it leads to countless misunderstandings and mountains of frustration on both sides. On the other hand, you probably know adults who seem to talk way too much!

Of course, some adults don't easily share their perspective. They're quiet and have their own thoughts, which might leave you wondering what they're thinking. Their reluctance to share might even send your monkey mind into overdrive as you try to fill in the blanks yourself. You may also be acquainted with the silent treatment as a way of punishing someone by not sharing feelings and thoughts, ignoring the other person altogether.

Then there is the element of how you speak, your "vocal presence." The tone, the pace, and the volume of your speech are relevant indicators as to your state of mind and your feelings about the topic, and they may even give some indication about your personality. If you want to be heard, the way you speak is highly relevant. As with so many things, balance is key. Speaking too fast is quickly interpreted as a sign of nervousness or even a lack of self-confidence. Talking fast can also make it appear that you don't believe people want to hear what you have to say. If you speak too slowly, people lose interest and engage with their monkey mind chatter quicker.

The tone of your voice can be a practical tool to convey your position on something, but use it in a thoughtful manner, without exaggerating. Also be mindful of verbal tics, such as "like" and "you know," as they can quickly turn off listeners. Building in frequent micropauses is an effective way to keep your listeners engaged.

SPEECH OFFERS CLUES

Your choice of words and tone of voice and the speed and emotion with which you speak are all clues the other person will use to determine what you believe and how you participate in the conversation. That's why it's superimportant to make sure that these various clues are fully aligned with what you internally feel and believe. People are surprisingly capable of (subconsciously) picking up on your inner experience and matching that to your words and behavior. If there is a mismatch between the two, they will draw harsh conclusions about you: untrustworthy, not real, not sincere... This makes congruence between your inner world and your outer expression a highly important aspect of mindful speaking.

How to Gather All Relevant Information Before You Speak

Of course, you and the other party both come into a difficult conversation with an opinion. You have ideas about the topic, and you may have experiences that support how you feel about it. Still, you both probably have more to say than just your preconceived opinion. As you've learned, a lot of the relevant information presents itself only during the conversation, and it is your job to dig around for any and all relevant information that's available under the surface so you can speak about it thoughtfully. Let's have a look at four ways to do that.

1. Conduct a Personal Check-In

What feelings, emotions, and memories are popping up inside you while you are having the talk offers you a lot of information about what's going on between you and the other person. Checking in with yourself is a great way to see if and how your inner experience (feelings and emotions) is correctly reflected in your outer expression (what you say and do).

Assess Congruence in Five Steps

To uncover information about this level of congruence, work from the outside (what the other person will notice about you) in (what you are experiencing within yourself). Here are the five steps:

1. Be fully present and notice how you are behaving and what you are saying.
2. Notice what energy you are bringing into the room. You can quickly scan your body for elements like lightheartedness versus heaviness and constructive and solution-driven versus trying to be right.
3. Check in with your body: How are you feeling on a physical level? Does your body feel at ease or tense? Is your breathing slow and deep or fast and shallow?
4. Move in deeper: What emotions are you experiencing? What is being triggered inside you?
5. Match the things you are experiencing on the inside (numbers 3 and 4) with what you are showing on the outside (numbers 1 and 2). Is there congruence between them? These four aspects should ideally be in alignment with each other, meaning that no aspect of your presence is outweighing another.

In Order to Align, Find Courage

If you notice that you are not yet fully aligned, what you need to fix that is courage. You need the courage to be open about what you are actually experiencing and share that with the other person. The way to do this is not by reacting mindlessly (for example, by screaming when you feel anger), but to talk about your feelings and thoughts as if they are a source of information. So instead of screaming, you can say something like "I notice that your last remark makes me angry."

The fourth way of gathering information, tapping into the undercurrent, will explain this further, but for now, simply acknowledge for yourself if you are not congruent in the conversation and be willing to change things.

2. Be Aware

The second way to gather information is to broaden your perspective and investigate outside yourself. How do you experience the energy in the room? What vibe are you picking up? What does that mean to you and how do you respond to that?

PICKING UP ON ENERGY

Without knowing it, you are probably already doing it: picking up and interpreting energy; for example, if you're meeting with a friend, you may sense immediately when you walk in that they're not in a good mood. But even in less obvious situations, there's interesting information available when you consciously scan the energy in the room. Try it out now: Close your eyes for a second and take a few deep breaths, breathing into your belly. Then slowly invite your energy to extend outward. First, send it directly around your own body, then a little farther out, into the room. What words, feelings, and emotions come up? Maybe the energy feels vibrant; maybe it's a little heavier. Try it out in a different place too. Experience the difference. Sensing energy is basically as simple as that. You just become consciously aware of the vibe in the room and use it as information, instead of brushing it aside.

Also, you investigate the other person: What vibe do they send out? Do you feel congruence between their energy and their words? How do they seem to be doing? What feelings do you pick up from them? You then evaluate: What is needed in this situation? What do you want to do with all the information that you collected? Sometimes this may lead to the realization that it's time to share your own perspective; sometimes it may seem better to ask a question.

3. Ask Questions

An obvious way to gather information during a conversation is to ask questions. You can ask questions to:

- Learn more about what the other person thinks or feels.
- Encourage them to explore a new perspective or see things from another angle.

The art of it is to find the right questions for the moment. Following are several useful types of questions and information about when they're best used in a mindful discussion.

Open-Ended Questions

An open-ended question is very broad and doesn't have a right or wrong answer to it. Asking an open-ended question is helpful to generate information to understand the other person better. The answer will give you insights into the other person's world. These types of questions are mainly valuable at the beginning of a difficult conversation when you are trying to get the various perspectives straight. Here are some examples:

- "Where would you like to go for dinner tonight?"
- "What is your favorite flower?"
- "How long have you been practicing medicine?"

Closed Questions

A closed question is a targeted question you can usually only answer with "yes" or "no," and it doesn't invite further response. A closed question generates little new information and may feel a little snappy, and because of that, you should be careful about when you ask one.

Nonetheless, asking closed questions can be very helpful, because they do create clarity. A yes/no question will establish whether or not the other person agrees with your statement or doesn't. When used sparingly and for the right reason, these types of questions can move the conversation further because they create a shared understanding. Try them at these points of a conversation:

- At the beginning, to establish a shared goal ("It's my intention to find a solution that works for both of us. Do you agree?").

- During the conversation, to summarize and check your understanding ("I've heard you explain...; did I get that right?").

- To wrap up the conversation, sometimes by making a new appointment ("Shall we continue our discussion next Thursday?").

"Why" Questions

"Why" is a superfast way to dive deep under the waterline, and it may help to uncover and clarify underlying reasons. "Why" questions lead to a much deeper layer within the other person's iceberg, and very often, the other person isn't at all ready or even willing to go there. In addition, "why" questions can come out as aggressive, leading, and hostile, like in the following examples:

- "Why do you behave like that?"

- "Why are you looking at me like that?"

- "Why are you upset?"

In response to a "why" question like these, you will often encounter defensive behavior, followed by counter questions, like "What do you mean?" or "Why do you want to know?" Needless to say, it's not helpful if you are hostile and your partner is defensive—these behaviors are highly counterproductive to connection and cooperation.

Think of "why" questions as the territory of coaches and therapists. In a supersafe environment, they can be acceptable, and very helpful, as a way to go deeper. In "normal" difficult conversations or conflicts, however, first try using an alternative:

- Try "What makes you_____," questions, like "What makes you do this?" or "What makes you believe that?"

- Check your assumptions or understanding of the other person by saying something like "I understand you behave like this because_____; is that right?"

Insightful Questions

The open-ended, closed, and "why" questions are categorized based on their form, but another way of looking at questions is to examine their aim. Very often when we ask questions, we ask them to satisfy our own curiosity. We ask questions to clarify things and give us more understanding (for example, "Who told you that?" or "Where would you like to move to?").

These sorts of questions can be very helpful in difficult conversations when we're in the phase of creating a better understanding of the facts and each other. Eventually, the facts are clear, and we need to progress to different types of questions.

At that point, we can move toward insightful questions, which create understanding for the other person. Unlike "why" questions, insightful questions won't be perceived as threatening. For example, when the other person is considering rational reasons for a decision, you may bring in the perspective of how they feel about the decision by asking something like "What makes you enthusiastic about it?" A question like that will offer a different way to look at the problem and create new insights into the situation for them. Of course, it creates new insight for you, too, but that isn't the primary goal. Insightful questions are often very empowering, too, and they may even help people shift from a victim or persecutor role into the empowered roles. Some of the other shifts insightful questions can create are:

- From problem to potential ("What would we need to be able to afford both?" instead of "Which option do you choose?").

- From narrow to broad ("Is this the real problem or is it actually something else?" instead of "What solution do you see?").

- From perspective to meaning ("What makes you think that?" instead of "What do you think about that?").

You can see how powerful insightful questions can be at pivotal points in a conversation because they usually show understanding, support, connection, and compassion, and they help move toward a solution.

4. Tap Into the Undercurrent

In Chapter 3, you learned a big chunk of the conversation's relevant information is hidden in the undercurrent. Now it's time to learn how to uncover that information and bring it up from the undercurrent into the actual conversation. There are two ways into the undercurrent.

- **You:** You can decide to share more of your own iceberg with the other person. You may feel nervous about this, and that's okay—but you'll learn why it's an effective way to invite connection and mutual understanding.

- **The other person:** It is also possible to bring up things you sense are going on in the other person's iceberg. This technique requires presence, awareness, and skill, and it should be done with respect for the other person's personal space.

Accessing the Undercurrent Through You

The first step in accessing the undercurrent is to be open about what is actually going on inside you when you are having the conversation, instead of covering that up (for example, with rational arguments). This starts by doing a personal check-in. Taking the time to notice what's going on with you will help you take the first step toward adding elements from the undercurrent to the conversation.

The openness required to uncover parts of your iceberg requires courage. And courage, unfortunately, is not something you will learn from a book, but instead it is like a muscle that you have to train in order for it to grow. Bringing up personal information from the undercurrent uncovers something about you that the other person may not yet know, and this is both why you don't want to do it and why you should do it anyway. Sharing truthful information about you deepens understanding and connection and leads to more successful conclusions.

Does this mean you have to share everything, like how you felt when you were dumped by your high school sweetheart? No! Even though that information might be relevant and useful for building connections in some conversations, it's not relevant when you're discussing a salary increase. On the contrary, sharing very personal information out of context is not at all helpful for easier conflict resolution.

Instead, share what you notice coming up for you during the exchange that is going on in that moment. For example, share how you feel undervalued because the increase in your payment has been pushed back yet another quarter. Share the irritation you feel when your boss isn't figuring out a way to prioritize it when she promised to last quarter.

Mindful Lesson:
Accessing the Undercurrent

Let's revisit Beth and Harry from Chapter 3 and their discussion about whom to invite to dinner the following week. (Harry would like to invite his mother, but Beth is opting for her friend Susan, who recently split from her longtime partner.) On the surface, this may seem like a rational, fact-based discussion, but in reality, both Beth and Harry have stuff going on under the surface.

For Beth especially, this conversation triggers a lot of things inside her iceberg. For example, she is noticing that she feels in touch with her core value that it's important to be there for friends in need. A little deeper down, it triggers her self-image of someone who is always kind and welcoming to people. Even deeper down, we find something else completely: her insecurity about how Harry's mom sees her. Every time Harry's mother is around, she worries that Harry's mother doesn't like her, and that worry sends her into a part of her personality that she doesn't particularly like.

Beth decides to dive in and share more about her true feelings, so she says: "There are a couple of reasons why I disagree with you on whom to invite. On the one hand, it has to do with wanting to be someone who is supportive when a friend needs help. On the other hand, I must admit that I feel insecure when your mother is around. I want her to like me so much, because she is important to you, but I feel I cannot live up to her high standards."

Harry is touched by Beth's words. Her honesty disarms him, and instead of pushing his suggestion so he can "win," he starts asking her questions as to how he could help her feel more confident around his mom. They conclude that, because Harry's mother is very important to him, it would be wise to invite her. Harry promises to challenge his mom's critical remarks and support Beth. They decide to invite Susan for dinner another time.

Accessing the Undercurrent Through the Other Person

The second way into the undercurrent is to bring up things you sense are going on in the other person's iceberg. This technique requires presence, awareness, and skill. When you are fully present with someone else, you naturally pick up signals about what is really going on for them, based on their energy level; the alignment between their words and their presence; and whether they are feeling calm, nervous, or even anxious.

For various reasons, this information is not often used in the actual conversation. Some people think:

- It is irrelevant.

- It is the other person's job to bring it out in the open.

- It is an infringement on the other person's privacy to even notice this, let alone make it part of the conversation.

- It is something that requires certain skills, which they lack, to bring up properly.

Despite these challenges, making this type of information part of the actual exchange can be one of the most helpful tools to move the conversation to a deeper, more meaningful level. When you bring something from the undercurrent into the conversation, you will help move your interaction in the right direction while also encouraging the other person to access and express their true feelings and beliefs about the topic.

At this point, you are still gathering information, but when it is time to speak, your use of what you pick up in the undercurrent will sound something like this: "I sense you are actually quite mad about this, right?" (even though you are not expressing that in your words) or "I feel there's a lot more to this, isn't there?" (than what you are currently sharing with me).

For people who are not naturally sensitive to other people's feelings, tapping into the undercurrent may seem challenging. And yes, it will probably take some practice to start getting a sense of what people are not explicitly sharing. But it all starts with being aware of the fact that there is more to explore. Your best way in is through being genuinely curious about the other person.

RESPECTING BOUNDARIES

When you try to access the other person's iceberg, make sure you aren't overstepping personal boundaries. Your intent and your way of speaking are how you prevent that. The basic ground rules are to engage with respect and compassion for the other person, to know for certain that you are and have been fully present the entire time, and to remind yourself of the intention to find a common way forward.

Recognizing What It's Really about Through the Undercurrent

Aside from sharing something about your own deeper motivations, beliefs, feelings, etc. or bringing up something you sense is going on with the other person, there's a third way you can use the undercurrent to deepen the conversation. Often, somewhere below the surface, there are hints about the way out of the difficulties you are experiencing. These come as meaningful coincidences, like sudden ideas popping up in one of the participants, an unexpected understanding, or a feeling that boils up. Summarized, you could call this "synchronicity."

Imagine, for example, being in a difficult conversation with your colleague about a shared assignment. She is the type of person who likes to follow the flow of things and works when inspiration strikes. You, however, like to make a timeline of everything that needs to be done. You two are debating which approach to take on your shared project, and the conversation doesn't seem to be going anywhere. Suddenly, a thought strikes you: What if you just plan out the project according to your system and mark three or four key milestones? If your colleague agrees to these milestones, what she does to get there won't matter that much. That way, both of you enjoy the pace of your own work rhythm, and you feel more confident about the chances of finishing in time and with the right deliverables. You suggest this to your colleague, and she embraces the thought. Together, you decide on the milestones and get to work.

In this example, a simple idea is the synchronicity that helps break through the deadlock you were in mere minutes ago. Be mindful of sudden thoughts, words, and feelings coming up, as they can be the way toward a workable solution. Many people ignore these, as they seem to be out of context or too obvious, but in fact they often are exactly what you are looking for. When you muster up the courage to mention your unexpected thought or feeling, you may be surprised about the effect!

Pitfalls to Avoid When Speaking

Once you've gathered relevant knowledge, it is time to start sharing your perspective on things. Let's explore six very common pitfalls in speech and how you can approach things in a mindful manner instead.

Pitfall: Attacking the Other Person
Mindful Approach: Offer Your Own Point of View

People have the tendency to stop listening and start defending when they feel attacked. It's a habit many of us have, but it's remarkable how fast the impact of anything you say drops when you get defensive.

Have a look at this sentence: "You should stop behaving like this."

Now look at the alternative: "It hurts my feelings when you do this."

The main difference is that in the second example, you approach the message from your own point of view, instead of pointing the finger at the other person.

The reason this technique works is twofold:

1. People generally don't feel the need to defend themselves when you say something about yourself. This opens their mind to actually reflect on what you're saying.

2. The parties won't get into an added dispute about whether or not what you say is correct. Because you said something about your own experience, it's not really possible to dispute it.

Pitfall: Spinning Endless Sentences
Mindful Approach: Pause After Your Initial Message

Some people go on and on in order to be sure they have included everything there is to say about the thing they're talking about. They might do this to prevent misunderstandings, but they also may do it to prevent the other person from having the ability to correct or add nuance or something else to their statement.

Unfortunately, the effect of this avalanche of words is that you're making your message more complicated and overwhelming. And that's not a good thing if you want to make connections and move forward. Also, wanting to prevent the other person from "scoring" is part of a win-lose strategy, not of the mindful approach to conflict resolution.

Instead, pause after you've given your initial message. This gives the other person the opportunity to contribute. If it turns out something wasn't clear, you can always clarify or make an addition.

Pitfall: Repeating Your Message in Different Words
Mindful Approach: Call Out Nonresponses

Simply rephrasing your message is something you would do when your message didn't get across the first time. In some cases, this may be what is needed, but most often, when someone isn't responding to what you (actually) said, it has to do with their unwillingness to do so and not with a lack of comprehension of your words.

Instead try something called "metacommunication," which means that you comment on what's going on in the conversation. If the other person isn't responding to your important statement, you could say something like "I feel you're not really responding to what I just said, but I do think it's very relevant. What's going on?" A question like that takes the conversation to another level, where you can (re)connect and try again.

Pitfall: Neutralizing Your Message
Mindful Approach: Speak Confidently

Neutralizing your message happens when you start by saying something pretty powerful but you get worried about the impact that might have, so you change course. Quickly, you decide to neutralize what you said by adding some "fluff." Fluff can be words; for example, you might say, "Really, I don't mean to say you're not doing it right, but..." or "Not to be unkind or anything..."

Fluff can also be a change in your behavior. This can be very subtle, like adding a little smile, shrugging, or literally shrinking yourself by bending down a bit or rolling your shoulders inward.

Neutralizing your message is not effective in a mindful conversation. It may seem like a kind way to alleviate some of the potential hurt in your message. But it is in fact quite confusing to the other person. It's much more honest to stand for what you've said. You then give the other person the opportunity to respond and work from there.

Pitfall: Filling the Silence
Mindful Approach: Respect Pauses

Filling the silence happens so often that you may not even recognize it as ineffective. But the truth is, silence can be a highly impactful and informative element of (difficult) conversations. As Leonardo da Vinci said, "Nothing strengthens authority so much as silence." After hearing what the other person has to say, it's good practice to take a breath and gather your thoughts. If, after you speak, the other person takes some time to respond, don't be scared of that silence. They may:

- Need time to gather their thoughts.
- Not yet know exactly how to say what they want to convey.
- Be gathering the courage to respond.

Respecting silence gives you an important tool in difficult conversations, as it allows new information to surface, both in yourself and in the other person.

Pitfall: Not Saying It
Mindful Approach: Speak Your Truth

This is the ultimate communication pitfall, and it happens all the time. Something is upsetting, hurtful, or disappointing to you, but instead of starting a conversation about it, you brush it aside.

We so often decide not to say anything to spare someone else's feelings, to prevent them from getting mad at us, or because we are afraid to speak our truth in general. As discussed in Chapter 1, there are two important reasons why this approach fails:

1. If you don't say it, you'll eventually show it.
2. If you don't say it, you're withholding from someone the opportunity to improve.

If something is upsetting you, the only way to deal with it is to start a conversation about it.

How to Speak Mindfully

Keeping the following key points in mind will help you speak in a way that is more likely to lead to positive solutions. They both build off the base of being fully present, speaking from the right intention, and using your curiosity to deepen your connection with the other person.

Be Sincere

Sincerity is a fundamental quality to speaking mindfully. It means that you are genuine, honest, and free from duplicity. Sincerity is where congruence between what you experience and what you say and do, the acceptance of your own vulnerability, openheartedness, and honesty all come together in one neat package. Sincerity cannot be faked, by definition. You can be sincere only if you believe in what you are saying. And if you believe in what you're saying, people will pick up on that and sense that you are acting genuinely. This atmosphere creates a broader shift in energy and an invitation for the other person to be sincere, too, which builds connection. If they accept the invitation, you've taken a huge step toward navigating your difficult conversation or conflict successfully.

SPEAK WITH CARE, NOT WITH CAUTION

Speaking with caution to protect feelings or reputations prevents you from speaking your truth. Speaking with care makes you try hard to be accurate and respectful and to stay connected.

Sincerity starts with intending to be sincere. Setting this intention involves the conscious choice to not be deceptive in your behavior or speech, and you honestly share your actual experience instead of some diluted form of it. This means disclosing information about your true self. When you do this, the other person can form an opinion about you that is based on who you really are and on your genuine beliefs about the situation.

Practice Kindness and Compassion

Mindful attitudes like generosity, kindness, and compassion can of course really shine in what you say and how you say it. Many people default to talking in absolutes (by saying words like "never" and "always"), but this approach doesn't support a constructive conversation. The other person's response to these kinds of statements will be to defend themselves and prove how the statements aren't true, leading the conversation away from the actual topic. Out of kindness and wisdom, refrain from using absolutes and instead talk about what you noticed in a specific situation.

Another common way of phrasing things, especially when you're in a tough discussion, is to use "but," as in "I understand what you are saying, but..." You may already know what happens when you hear that "but": Everything that was said before it is wiped out. Everyone assumes that the most important message will be coming after the "but." Alternatively, you can use "and," as in "I heard what you are saying, and I would like to add..." "And" is inclusive, as you've seen in the And Stance: Both things can be just as right, which is very supportive to mindful mindsets like win-win, generosity, and being open to synchronicity.

Give the other person the benefit of the doubt by acknowledging their experience (which doesn't mean you have to agree with them) and by being mindful of the fact that how you have experienced the things they said or did isn't necessarily how they were meant. Impact and intention are not always the same (for example, "The way you spoke to me made me feel attacked, even though I know that wasn't your intention.").

Mindful Lesson:
Bringing It Together

Mark is the CEO of a clean-tech start-up. He is leading a group of driven young professionals, and among them is Sam. Sam is ambitious and really good at his job, but Mark feels he isn't performing at the peak of his potential. Mark knows he has to have a chat with Sam to find out what's going on.

Mark will be bringing up the topic during today's one-on-one with Sam. Right before their meeting starts, he puts aside his other work and shifts his attention to the upcoming talk. He sets an intention of wanting to find out why Sam isn't giving his all, and if possible, find a way to motivate Sam more. When Sam enters the room, Mark is aware of a shift in energy: There is a tension present that wasn't there before. He checks in with himself again to find out what the effect of Sam's entrance is. He realizes his positive intention is sliding a little, as it is now mixed with confusion and even some irritation about Sam's vibe. He takes a deep breath and consciously decides to stay positive and open.

Mark welcomes Sam, and they chat briefly about their weekends. Then Mark says that he's noticed Sam's declining input and mentions his feeling that Sam isn't giving his all. He asks, "Do you recognize this?" Sam shrugs and says he's not sure. Mark briefly describes two examples where Sam didn't spend enough time on a project to really make it work, and the projects weren't finished as well as they could have been. Mark wants to ask, "Why have you been cutting corners?" but catches himself because that question will push Sam into a defensive mode. Mark rephrases to an open-ended question instead: "What do you think about the way you handled these projects?"

Sam considers his response. He says, "I think I did a pretty good job, maybe not the best ever, but pretty good."

Mark checks in with himself again: he notices his irritation rising. He suddenly realizes that what is happening in the conversation is a beautiful illustration of what he senses in Sam: It's all pretty good but not the best ever—just how Sam is now answering questions but is not really invested in the conversation. He says, "I notice that you don't seem to be all in, not in the projects and not in this conversation. What is going on? You used to be my best guy."

This is a bold move: Mark is bringing up what's happening in the under-current of the conversation, and this may trigger Sam to open up, or to withdraw further. Luckily, Mark's sincerity and honest curiosity reach Sam, and he nods: "I know; I've been starting to have doubts about whether this job is right for me. It doesn't challenge me as much as it did, and without the challenge, I start slacking." This is where they need to be. Now that it's on the table, they can explore how they want to proceed. Mark has plenty of challenging projects Sam could take on if he is willing to go all the way again. They agree on a period after which they will evaluate if Sam's back on track now that he'll have some new challenging stuff to work on, but both feel confident that he will be.

Starting Small

Much of what most people need to practice with regard to mindful speaking is how to access the undercurrent in a compassionate way. You might want to begin by growing your awareness of what is happening in the undercurrent a little further by checking small things with the people you are talking with. So, for example, in a normal conversation with your partner about where to go to dinner, use the unspoken signals they send out to say something like "I get the feeling that you especially want to eat somewhere we haven't been before; is that right?"

Developing mindful speaking is easiest when you approach it as an exploration or a little adventure. Just being curious about the undercurrent will make you want to check in with yourself and others. It will definitely take practice, but you will grow your confidence quickly if you just start small.

Practice Experiencing Sincerity

In the meantime, there's no harm in starting to speak with sincerity today. Speaking with sincerity is a powerful experience. Knowing you are saying what is really, really true for you diminishes the stress of being in a challenging situation. It lowers the focus on what the other person might think about what you say, as it is so clearly true for you.

You could say that sincerity is an easy win. We can all do it already; it's just a matter of choosing to do so. Some people even notice when they speak with sincerity that they experience a feeling of positive energy flowing through them.

Let's try that out: Sit in a chair with your feet on the ground. Place your left hand on your heart and your right hand on your belly. Bring your attention to your breathing first; breathe into your belly, connecting to your body. Then bring your attention to something you know is true for you, like how much you value your job or how much you appreciate your house. Really go into that feeling, connect to it, and breathe into it. And become aware of the energetic sensations you experience in your midriff. This feeling is one you will get used to experiencing when you speak mindfully in difficult conversations.

CHAPTER SUMMARY

The following are takeaways, action steps, and reminders to help you on your journey toward mindful speaking.

● Mindful speakers know that their perspective matters. They are willing and open to share how they see things. They know how to avoid the challenges that speaking can bring by fully owning their perspective on the situation. They are not afraid to accept their part of the story and are completely sincere in their speech, allowing their true self to be seen. This may lead to vulnerability, and mindful speakers are okay with that.

● There are four different ways of gathering more information: doing a personal check-in, broadening your awareness, asking different kinds of questions, and tapping into the undercurrent. Each of them has its own value, and ideally you'll use all four to some degree in every hard conversation to make as much information as possible available to you.

● You learned how to avoid the most common pitfalls, like attacking people, going on too long, and filling up silences. You have also learned to be conscious in the words you choose and your tone of voice by adopting sincerity and kindness.

● You learned to pick up much more than what is literally being said both in yourself and in others. You also learned to use this to bring the conversation to a deeper level. This will help both you and the other person to access information in your icebergs about your beliefs, values, and emotions around the topic or situation, making it possible to discuss the things that really matter.

CHAPTER 7
THE PAUSE APPROACH

"Truth and courage aren't always comfortable,
but they're never weakness."

Brené Brown

In the previous three chapters, you have learned the skills to being, listening, and speaking in difficult conversations. And in Part 1 of this book, you have learned the basic principles to thoughtfully handling your confrontations. It can feel like a big responsibility when you realize how you can, and need to, influence conversations. There is so much to think about, so much to be and do, and so much to notice.

No need to fear, though! In this chapter you'll learn the mnemonic PAUSE, which brings the whole mindful approach to conflict resolution together in an easy-to-remember, step-by-step system. You will also learn what to do when others don't play by the rules, how to approach toxic personalities, and how to invite people into a mindful conversation about tough topics.

The PAUSE Approach

In the PAUSE approach, the mindset and skills you've learned in this book come together in an easy-to-remember way. Following the five steps of PAUSE will help free you from responding out of fear and old pain. PAUSE opens you to a positive and productive mindset while engaging all of you, bringing out everything relevant to the conversation, allowing you to recognize potential solutions or ways out when they come up. PAUSE is an acronym, and each letter stands for a broader concept. However, even the word "pause" itself will most likely be enough to help you remember that broader concept while following the five steps. PAUSE stands for:

Presence

Acceptance

Undercurrent

Synchronicity

Exchange

The PAUSE approach is a circular process. After you've shared what you wanted to say and the other person is responding, you return to step one, allowing new information to reach you.

The fact that using the PAUSE approach will remind you to pause is an added advantage. Taking a moment to pause can do wonders for your ability to handle a difficult situation or person. Take a deep breath and allow yourself just enough time to regroup and consider how you want to be in this confrontation: Do you choose to judge? Do you make them see you are right? Or do you choose to engage with awareness and find a way forward that works? As Gerald Jampolsky, a world-renowned authority on psychiatry and health, says: "You can be right, or you can be happy."

Let's explore each word in PAUSE to see the broader concept it represents.

Presence

The primary trait of mindful awareness, and of the PAUSE approach, is to stay fully present during each and every moment of your interaction.

- Cut out all distractions.

- Let go of the monkey mind chatter about the past, the future, and what exactly to say next. Be here, now.

- Discover how the other person is behaving in this moment.

- Think about what you are learning about their reasons and needs, as well as what you are learning about your own reasons and needs.

Your personal presence also includes the energy you bring into a conversation. Focusing on personal presence is a conscious decision to create a strong alignment between your inner and outer worlds, which will have a positive influence on the strength and trustworthiness you project.

Acceptance

Your acceptance of the situation and the other person as they are right now is a crucial step to take in mindful conflict management. It won't be possible to see the potential solutions that are emerging without taking this step first. From there on out, it's easier to allow the process to unfold as it does, without striving to reach a specific solution, and without judging the other person, the situation, or yourself. You're basically letting go of the need for anything particular to happen and taking a step back into an observer position.

By being less emotionally invested in a specific outcome, it's possible to keep an open mind about the surprises the conversation has in store for you. And more than anything, it'll help to bring your curiosity and a beginner's mind to the situation, so you actively search for new insights about the situation, the other person, or yourself.

Undercurrent

You open up your awareness of the undercurrent of the conversation through being:

- Present in the conversation and in your own body.

- Able to sense more than people say.

- Able to notice subtle shifts in energy.

The skills you've learned in this book make the undercurrent—and its treasure trove of useful information—available to you. Use it to help you to find compassionate words and make constructive suggestions to move the conflict forward in a positive way.

Synchronicity

Your connection to the undercurrent opens you to the potential of synchronicity. Expect to be pleasantly surprised, and you probably will be. Essential here is bringing in the mindsets of interconnection and win-win, trusting the process, and believing that a positive way forward will come up. Keep in mind that what is really important will present itself during the conversation itself, not while preparing.

Be very mindful of what happens during the conversation. Quite often you'll find that the reason you are having the conversation in the first place is also playing itself out in the talk you're having. So if you feel annoyed or irritated, look at what's going on, and maybe you can use what is happening now as an illustration of what is happening in the broader sense.

By simply acknowledging and acting on the unexpected ideas that emerge when you allow your true self to meet their true self, the best way forward or that crucial thing to say may miraculously spring to mind. So to paraphrase Wayne Dyer, be realistic, expect miracles.

Exchange

This final step in the PAUSE approach is about your actual exchange with the other person. Saying what you have to say in a mindful way is a very powerful tool. This is where you bring everything you've gathered, found, feel, know, and wish into form (through mindful speaking). It's important to say what you want to say in the sincerest way possible. Speaking with sincerity is the manifestation of a strong alignment between your inner world and your words. Through hearing your words, the other person will know what you are all about.

MINDFULNESS IS HEARTFULNESS

In many Asian languages, the word for "mind" is the same as the word for "heart." In his 2010 talk at the Greater Good Science Center at the University of California, Berkeley, Jon Kabat-Zinn described mindfulness as "presence of heart." A mindful approach to conflict resolution, at its core, has everything to do with being connected to one's heart.

By trusting the process and engaging with it fully, you also bring your power in. However tough a situation may be and however difficult or long-standing the conflict, never forget that you are the co-owner of it. You are not weak; you are no victim. You have the power to influence the way this conversation is going and the outcome of it.

Apply PAUSE to a Past Conversation to Practice

To see where your mindful conflict management skills currently stand, spend some time analyzing a few recent challenging conversations. You probably remember at least a couple.

Create some quiet time and space for yourself to do this exercise. Bring a pen and paper to capture your thoughts. Think of a challenging conversation—one from your private life or a professional experience.

Sit comfortably, with both feet on the ground, and breathe into your belly to center yourself in your body. Think back to what happened and explore by going over each step of the PAUSE approach: Were you completely present all the time or were there distractions? Did you take time in the beginning of and during the conversation to check in with yourself and connect to what you were experiencing? Did you take account of your energy and your presence?

Were you able to accept the situation as it was? Could you let go and explore or were you striving to create a specific outcome? Were you open to tap into the undercurrent? Did you do anything with the signals you picked up from the other person or the intuitive hunches you found in yourself? Did you recognize the synchronistic or unexpected ideas for what they were? Did you bring them into the conversation to explore if they may have been an interesting way forward? Did you speak with sincerity and were you fully accepting of your ownership of the situation?

Conduct this postmortem for at least three difficult conversations in your past. You'll probably start to see patterns and recognize which elements come naturally to you and which ones require a little more practice and awareness.

Take the skills that require your attention and begin your practice of the PAUSE approach with them. In your upcoming conversations (they don't even have to be conflicts), consciously focus on one part of the PAUSE approach you find challenging. After it becomes easier for you to use each of the steps by itself, begin to add the other steps, until you can use all five steps of PAUSE in one conversation.

If It Doesn't Go Well

Now you know how to manage conflicts mindfully, so all will be well. Right?

We all know the world doesn't work that way. What if you get entangled in a difficult conversation and even though you try to follow PAUSE, it just isn't working? There are two potential reasons for that: It's either you or it's them. Either you get stuck somewhere, or they aren't playing the same game. Let's explore how to deal with both potential scenarios.

Could It Be You?

As you know by now, start by checking in with yourself:

- Are you fully present?
- Have you accepted the situation as it is, so you can be open to what it might become?
- Are you open to what is happening in the undercurrent?
- Are you open to synchronicities?
- Are you using what is happening in the undercurrent and the potential synchronicities to steer the conversation to the topics that really matter?

If the answer to any of these questions is "no," that's where you start adjusting. As long as the conversation is going on, you can go ahead and make a shift in how you are showing up.

If the answer to all of these questions is positive, however, you'll have to investigate further:

- What is really going on inside you?
- Are your words in full alignment with what you are experiencing inside?
- Why are things getting intense for you?
- Are you speaking your full truth?
- Are you disclosing how you really feel?

If you notice that somewhere you are not in full integrity, ask yourself why. What is keeping you from really opening up? Of course, there may be many reasons why you do not feel safe to open up completely. Some of them can be handled by adding courage and doing it anyway. But there are a few reasons that are worth some extra attention.

You Fear Escalation

Maybe you notice that the situation is on the brink of escalation. Strong emotions are rising within either one of you, maybe even both of you, and you feel uncertain about your ability to contain the situation. This uncertainty may keep you from expressing what you really feel about the situation. So how do you work with that?

First of all, remind yourself that you know how to handle emotions, and there is nothing to be scared of. Take a few breaths and then talk about the emotions instead of letting them play out entirely on a physical plane. This one moment of breathing is enough to defuse the situation. But if you didn't catch yourself in time, and emotions are spilling over, that's not the end of the world. As soon as you have regrouped even a little bit, name what is going on with you: "I am just so saddened by all this" or "Your remark really hit a nerve with me," for example.

If the strong emotions are the other person's, you may want to consider if it could actually be helpful to allow the emotional balloon to pop. Allowing the emotions to be expressed is sometimes the most straightforward way to work through a tough situation, even when the emotion is anger and it's pointed at you. In a situation like this, it's wise to consider if the release of emotions will support a positive outcome. If so, it's often enough to name the emotion you're picking up to release it: "I see you are angry..." is an example.

In handling emotions, the most important thing to remember is that they are just an accumulation of feelings. Be compassionate when they come up, both for the other person and yourself.

Ask Yourself If You Should Apologize

If you reacted from your emotions (whether in this conversation or an earlier one), or if you did something else that has hurt or harmed the other person, remember the power of a true apology. Some people find it really difficult to apologize, but it can be the very best thing to do.

After all, everyone makes mistakes. We are all fallible. And maybe you didn't mean something to happen or you didn't intend to hurt someone, but apparently it did happen and someone did get hurt. Impact is not the same as intent, and it's wise to embrace that. You do not have to tell someone they are right or their interpretation of what happened is correct to make amends for the apparent impact you've had on them.

You're Confronted with a Source of the Conflict

Quite often, the reason why you are having the conversation will play itself out during the conversation. The fact that you are being confronted with the very thing that makes this person troublesome to begin with may challenge or scare you, making it hard to handle the situation in a thoughtful manner. But you have tools for dealing with this scenario: Refer to the present moment to explain what's difficult for you. That's one of the most powerful ways to discuss challenging things with people.

Mindful Lesson:
Working with What Is Happening Now

Tania and her brother Jamal cannot seem to get on the same page on anything. They are constantly bickering about small things. Tania is sad about this. She loves Jamal and would like to spend more time with him, but these constant disagreements suck energy from her. She has mustered the courage to have a talk with Jamal about this, but even finding the time to meet has been tough.

Now that they are finally in the same room, they have already had small clashes about where to sit and when they last met. Tania is feeling desperate. How can they have a meaningful talk about this when they cannot even seem to be able to agree on things like that?

When Tania checks in with herself, she realizes she is feeling so upset because she's actually in the middle of what brought her to this meeting: their inability to simply agree on things. She wonders why this started in the first place; they used to get along just fine.

She decides to take what is right in front of her as a way into the conversation. "Jamal, I feel we are constantly fighting over really small things, like right now: We cannot agree on something as simple as the best place to sit in this café. What do you think is going on?" By simply referring to something that was happening a minute ago, Tania cleverly averts Jamal remembering things differently. Jamal hesitates.

His first response is to contradict Tania, but he catches himself because of her open-ended and sincere question. He hears she really wants to know what he's thinking from her tone of voice and open attitude. He says, "I see what you mean. I remember we started doing this when we were teenagers. On my end, I think I started doing it because you are my big sister... I didn't want to always agree with you."

Tania considers this. His explanation resonates with her. She says, "Wow, thank you, I see what you mean! I never thought of it that way, but maybe that's why it started with me too: Being the big sister, I needed to be right in a way."

After this moment, they further discuss how they want their relationship to be, now that they are adults and no longer need to rival each other. What worked in the past doesn't necessarily work in the present or the future, so they agree to make changes.

You're Experiencing Accusations and Verbal Attack

A final reason why you may not fully unveil what's going on for you is because you feel verbally attacked. If the other person starts name-calling or making accusations, do not be afraid to set boundaries.

Mindful conflict resolution does not mean that you should let people walk all over you. It's completely acceptable—and advisable—to be clear when they are crossing a line. You can set boundaries by framing things from your perspective and not by launching a counterattack. You could even use some iceberg material to build a stronger connection: "I feel attacked by the way you phrase this, and that makes me close off to you. Could you please rephrase what you want to say to me?"

Could It Be the Other Person?

If you've (quickly) checked all of these reasons why you could be out of alignment, and it turns out you're not, then, and only then, it is time to look across the table. Maybe it is the other party after all.

Invite People In

In most situations, when you embrace the PAUSE approach, you will automatically invite the other person into mindfully handling the conversation. Your way of being, your responses, and your overall mindset will diffuse most negativity. But sometimes they won't.

TALKING TO OTHERS ABOUT MINDFULNESS

When you are in the middle of a tough situation, it's not usually a good time to start explaining a new concept. Explaining something new takes time and attention away from the difficult situation itself, and most of the time, your partner in the disagreement will not appreciate that. Instead, see if you can introduce a mindful approach to important people in your life when there is no dispute in sight. You could discuss it as a way to deal with future challenges. At work, the PAUSE approach can be part of a team alignment session.

When you notice that, even though you have been wholeheartedly working with the mindset and tools from this book, your partner in the dispute is still basically picking a shallow, fact-based fight with you, here are some things you can try.

- When someone is staying on a superficial or a content level, but you feel there are deeper reasons for your trouble, it may be helpful to invite them to share their perspective on another level (for example: "I feel we are staying at the surface—should we explore what is going on on a deeper level?").

- If the other person is accusing you of doing something wrong or of not understanding them, a smart, yet unorthodox, way to bring them into a constructive talk is to embrace curiosity. Invite them to share more of their take on things so you can further explore their standpoint. You could ask something like "Could you maybe tell me more about this so I better understand?" Of course, you'll be speaking sincerely, and that will come across in your tone. Since people have a need to be heard, being invited to vent can really help clear the air. If you can be okay with them explaining what you did wrong, and why, without becoming defensive or closed off, in the longer run, you might have done a really supportive thing for all involved. You will allow them to just talk it out, and you will learn a lot about their underlying motives and beliefs. Of course, you can ask questions to clarify and maybe to help them gain a deeper insight. After you've heard them out, follow PAUSE to give an honest response.

- Sometimes it's helpful to talk about what you see happening by using "metacommunication." "Meta" indicates that this type of communication is saying something about the communication itself—it's self-referential. So if the two of you are bickering or you feel the conversation is spiraling unhelpfully, you could say something like "I feel we are moving away from a productive conversation. How about setting a few ground rules together?" (Offer suggestions, like allowing each other first to share their full story, and then focus on finding a solution.)

If People Show Toxic Behavior

Some people are really challenging to handle because they display toxic behavior. You probably know at least a few people in whose company you start feeling drained, annoyed, or even sad. Toxic people are everywhere, and they come in many different varieties. They may be narcissistic, want to complain about everything, focus solely on negativity, be gossipy, be prone to drama, put an emotional claim on you, or act like they know everything. The easiest way to recognize them is by taking note of how you feel after you've spent time with them. If you only feel a little low on energy once, that can be chance. If it happens twice, you get into the risky zone, and when it happens three times or more, it's a pattern.

The biggest risk in handling toxic people is to think that you can change them, or to hope that they will change themselves, and to stay in the relationship longer than is wise for your own well-being. Another risk is to spend so much time mulling over just how problematic your toxic person is that you get sucked into negativity all by yourself. Handling toxic people requires (a) acknowledging to yourself that you're dealing with a toxic person (the awareness will help you pause, instead of jumping to an immediate response), (b) being completely realistic about the fact that people hardly ever change (unless they see the value of it themselves—mindful tenet: acceptance), and (c) focusing on how to deal with them instead of spending your time thinking about how horrible they are (mindful tenet: nonjudgment).

In interacting with toxic people, it's really hard to stay away from emotionally responding to their appeal to acknowledge them. In your interactions with them, try these strategies.

1. **Accept that they are as they are at this point in time.** Acceptance is key here. This will leave you with a choice: Do you want to spend more time in the company of toxicity or are you ready to go?
2. **Set clear boundaries and limits if you decide to continue talking.** To your narcissistic friend, you could say, "I have heard

a lot about how things are going with you, and I really appreciate you sharing so much. There has been a lot going on in my life, too, and it's important for me to share some of my experiences with you. Are you open to listening to me for a bit?" And to a friend who gossips a lot you might be quite direct and say something like "I don't really like to talk about others when they can't defend themselves. But if you want, we can discuss how to bring up this topic with them to clear the air between you."

3. **Use the drama triangle and empowerment dynamic.** Some toxic people can be approached using what you learned about these in Chapter 3. Complainers, for example, are basically putting themselves in the victim position. By asking them what they are planning to do to change things, or maybe what sort of support they would need to make the necessary changes, you invite them to step out of the drama triangle. Even though many times they won't be able to make a change yet, sticking with this strategy will allow you to avoid either saving them or becoming the persecutor.

A Golden Partnership: Sincerity and Curiosity

When the going gets tough—whether it's you or the other person who's having a tough time—what you really need to remember is to embrace sincerity and curiosity. This golden duo of "mindsets" is part of the PAUSE approach, but even when all other elements of the mindful approach have momentarily sunk to the background of your mind, these two will keep you on the mindful side of things.

Sincerity

Being sincere in a conversation is to say only things that you believe are completely true and to constantly speak from a state of congruence between what you say and what you are experiencing on the inside. To be sincere, you need to be aware of and okay with yourself—both the things you like about yourself and the things you are less happy with. It's also important to lower your guard in order to uncover truths about yourself. In situations where things are hard, this can be superchallenging and scary, but when you speak with sincerity, your message has much more of an impact.

Sincerity is found in a combination of the choice of words, inner alignment, and tone of voice. It's hard to script, and the simplest way to know what to say is to take a step back, breathe into your abdomen, and ask, "What is really true for me right now?" You may realize that what is really true leads to saying something like "You know, at this point what I really want is to just be able to move past this and be friends again. What do you think would be needed to do that?" Speaking with sincerity softens the other person considerably, which will create a new opening to pick up the conversation on a more constructive level.

Curiosity

Curiosity is the other essential state to embrace when things are heating up. It is the powerhouse of cooperation and interconnection, and when conversations turn difficult, curiosity will keep you on the mindful side of things instead of falling into traps like defensiveness and protecting your ego.

MOVING ON VERSUS FORGETTING

Deciding to move on doesn't mean that you have to be okay with everything that happened in the past, nor do you have to forget it. It does mean that you may be able to set aside past hurts for the time being and be present with what is happening now. When you are capable of putting aside what has happened in the past in favor of what is happening right now, you can allow everything you are right now to meet everything the other person is right now, and see how this influences the situation.

Being curious will remind you to wonder why things are so problematic. Curiosity works both ways: It will drive you to ask questions of the other person and of yourself as well. What is being stirred in both of your icebergs that makes things so hard? Curiosity holds a powerful energy of learning, growing, and looking toward the future, which overrides judging, history, and old opinions. It brings you into the present moment. Being curious will invite you to ask, "Why do you experience it that way?" instead of blurting out: "That's so unfair!"

Mindful Lesson:
Being Curious

Margaret has had a challenging relationship with her father, John, since she was young. John and Margaret's mother got divorced when Margaret was in high school, and since then, John has been more or less absent from her life. Margaret had a good childhood, but the fact that her father was hardly there for her definitely left some marks.

Margaret has been very angry with her father, but lately she's beginning to realize that staying angry will not make her any happier. She also realizes that she doesn't want him to be out of her life completely. She has decided to talk with him to learn more about his perspective, as she never really understood the whys: Why did he do things the way he did? Why did he not take more initiative to see her? And how does he see their past and their future? She believes that answers to these questions will help her make more sense of things and might lead to a communal future instead of drifting further apart.

When she's meeting her father, she's all set to use the PAUSE approach, but very quickly she notices he isn't. He's accusing her of never visiting or calling. Margaret is taken completely off guard by this, but instead of getting into defensive mode, she takes a deep breath and centers herself, strengthening her presence. She remembers the power of sincerity and curiosity. She says, "Dad, I am completely taken aback by your words. They hurt and surprise me in equal measure after all the years you haven't been there for me." She allows her words to sink in and sees how her father is a little startled. She then says, "But to be honest, I am here to learn more about your perspective, and I am very curious: How were things for you when Mom and you were first divorced?"

Even though she's saddened and hurt by her father's lack of consideration, she focuses on her intention to learn about his story. Her sincerity and her willingness to hear his side of the story shift her father's accusing approach. He seems to like to talk about his side of things, and since Margaret is willing to hear him out, his demeanor softens considerably, allowing them to finally explore how they can be in each other's lives from now on.

When you engage in difficult conversations with sincerity when you speak and with curiosity when you listen, you create a self-reinforcing flow in the conversation, which makes it almost impossible for the conversation to get out of hand. Making a statement that is completely sincere and uncovers a truth about you, followed by asking a genuinely curious question to learn more about the other person's needs, disarms the other person. This strategy has such a positive energy to it that it tends to bring a conversation back on track.

CHAPTER SUMMARY

The following are takeaways, action steps, and reminders to help you on your journey toward mindful speaking.

- Don't expect things to feel comfortable right away. Learning something new always takes time.

- It can be pretty intense to disclose things you would normally hide from others. Yet it is worth the effort because it helps to share your mindful journey and your new approach with the people who are close to you. That way, you build a support system, and others will understand when you're suddenly trying new things. Also, it's perfectly fine to take it slow and allow yourself time to practice to build a strong foundation.

- PAUSE is an acronym, standing for the following words "presence," "acceptance," "undercurrent," "synchronicity," and "exchange." By following the five steps of PAUSE, you will keep focused on the mindful tenets that will consistently bring you back to the core steps you want to take.

- If you're trying to use PAUSE and find it's not working, always check in with yourself first: Are you really doing everything in your power to make this conversation a mindful one? If there's really nothing left for you to change, then it's time to see what the other person might be doing that makes it hard to stay on the mindful side of things.

- Allowing emotions to surface and be visible is not a bad thing. In some cases, it's wisest to defuse the situation, but in others, it's better to let the emotions run their course. Trust your gut on this: You will know when it's better to stoke the fire and when it's better to cool it.

- The golden partnership is a quick way to put situations that seem to be getting out of hand back on track. Making a statement that is completely sincere and uncovers a truth about you, followed by a genuine, curious question to learn more about the other person's needs, will create a positive flow that tends to bring a conversation back on track.

PART 3

HOW TO APPLY PAUSE IN REAL LIFE

In this third part, you'll focus on using the PAUSE approach in common, real-world situations. This method can be used in both your professional and private life, so you will learn the specifics to applying the approach in the relationships with your partner (Chapter 8), your family (Chapter 9), your friends (Chapter 10), and your coworkers (Chapter 11).

Feel free to skip around within this part to visit the sections most pertinent to you at this point. The chapters in this part follow the same structure, which makes them easy to navigate. First, they explore what makes difficult situations in this type of relationship specifically challenging. Second, they discuss how the PAUSE approach can support you in handling the difficult situations you may walk into. And finally, there are a couple of common examples of challenging situations and how you can best handle these using the mindful approach to conflict resolution.

CHAPTER 8
USING THE PAUSE APPROACH WITH YOUR PARTNER

> "The ultimate test of a relationship
> is to disagree but to hold hands."
>
> *Alexandra Penney*

It's possible that people have the most difficult conversations in romantic relationships. Maybe with the exception of your parents when you were young, your expectations aren't quite as high in any other relationship. It's so tempting to think of your partner as the one person who should make you complete, happy, and whole—that's why people expect their partners to be everything, all of the time. The bar is set so high that it is basically humanly impossible to deliver for just one person. This in itself accounts for a whole lot of difficult conversations and conflicts, some of which will be explored in this chapter. Everywhere you are not yet fully okay with yourself is where your partner will trigger you. The tips in this chapter will help you stay grounded and secure even when things with your significant other are tough, and they will assist you in keeping the atmosphere positive, constructive, and lighthearted.

The Challenges of Difficult Conversations in Romantic Love

Romantic love can be beautiful, life-affirming, and magical, but it can also be incredibly challenging. It's often challenging because to make the relationship with your significant other really work, a lot of stuff needs to be cleared out of each other's iceberg. No one can be perfect in every sense all of the time—not you, not your partner. This realization might be a hard one to swallow, but embracing it will make some space to see the person you are actually with instead of looking at them through a lens of expectations, assumptions, and fears.

No One Can Make You Whole (Except You)

One of the most painful misconceptions in romantic relationships is that your partner will make you whole—meaning that they, and only they, will make you feel secure, loved, and happy. This (subconscious) assumption makes discussing topics that may already be quite hard even harder. For your partner, logically, it will be challenging to live up to the high expectations you have of them. For you, it's probably going to be tough to see that your expectations aren't always met.

Ideally, both of you would feel secure, loved, and happy all by yourself, but in plenty of good relationships, one or both partners are still working on getting to that point. And to an extent, still being on that journey is completely fine. However, when people do not take full responsibility for their own personal development, all eyes are on the partner to validate, love, and bring safety and security. If any of these needs are not met, arguments based on jealousy, loneliness, and fear can result.

No One Can Read Your Mind

Another reason it can be really hard to work through challenges with your significant other is because you may expect them to be able to read your mind. But even very empathic people won't be able to do that. To make sure your partner knows what you need from them, be it in emotional matters, the household chores, or time spent together, you will have to tell them.

This may seem logical now, but imagine all the moments when you in some way assume you'll be understood without actually stating what's on your mind. It leads to lots of irritation and even anger when things you assumed were clear turn out not to be clear at all. Being open about your expectations clears the air and allows for agreements to be made based on a mutual understanding instead of assumptions.

Encountering Old Pain

In mindfully approaching difficult conversations, uncovering more of your iceberg and allowing yourself to be vulnerable is a crucial step toward building interconnection and mutual trust. Yet, if you have been hurt before or you're just really scared of being hurt, this step will be especially challenging. This doesn't make it easier to have the talks that matter. If you are constantly protecting yourself from being hurt, you prevent interconnection from happening. Without interconnection, it is very difficult to talk about the undercurrent. And without getting into the undercurrent, it's hard to figure out what is really important to each of you, find common ground, and work toward shared solutions.

You Can Work to Improve Your Relationship

No relationship is perfect all the time. Even though you may have found a great partner, that doesn't mean it'll be smooth sailing from now on. Something as important as your relationship can't be left to chance. Any relationship requires conscious attention, investment of time and energy, and plenty of open and mindful communication. There are many ways to invest in your relationship, and one of them is to consciously create opportunities to discuss the topics that are important to one or both of you. Preferably, you won't wait until these (often emotionally charged) topics are posing concrete challenges in your life—instead deliberately talk about them before they have a chance of getting out of hand. For example, it's clearly less stressful to discuss if you want to have children together before you get pregnant.

THE FIVE LOVE LANGUAGES

According to Gary Chapman in his 1992 book *The Five Love Languages: How to Express Heartfelt Commitment to Your Mate*, there are five different love languages, or ways different people feel loved and appreciated. Depending on your individual personality type, you may feel loved differently than how your partner does. See the Online Resources section at the back of this book for a referral to the website where you'll find descriptions of each love language and a helpful test.

Love Is Different in Different Phases of Your Life

Whether you are in college or trying to climb the corporate ladder, or whether you have children living with you or are empty nesters, things are different in different phases of your life. Your current reality is always reflected in your relationship. It's important to reevaluate how you want to be together in any new phase of life by discussing the topics that matter most again when you expect a transition.

How the Mindful Approach Will Support You

When you are looking to find connection, intimacy, passion, and love, you need to stop responding from fear, pain, past hurts, defensiveness, and shielding. Love and the mindful approach to conflict resolution are truly made for each other. By taking the five steps of the PAUSE approach when speaking with your partner, you will make sure you are fully present with them, are aware of the mindset that will support your connection, use the skills you've developed to uncover what's going on in the undercurrent, and recognize when synchronicities occur. In your exchange, allow sincerity, curiosity, and interconnection to be your guides.

Presence

When discussing the challenges you face with your life partner, with whom you may share a household and maybe even a family, it's important to really be present with them. There may be a thousand things pulling your attention away from the subject at hand—kids running around, dishes piling up, text messages pinging—but when your partner is engaging you in a talk about something they find hard, you need to be there with them. It's really unhelpful to be handling practicalities around the house in the meantime, so find a time when you can focus solely on the matter at hand.

Acceptance

In difficult moments with your partner, it is important to look at the facts as they are and accept them, instead of allowing any stories you may be spinning in your head to take over. You may be creating stories on how things probably are/were/will be, or how they should be or become. If, for example, you saw your girlfriend chatting with another man in a bar one night, you may immediately start spinning a story of how she is done with you and wants to see other people.

Is this true? There's only one way to find out: Have a talk about it. By keeping your open mind, embracing beginner's mind and being curious, and letting go of your imaginary story when having a conversation with her, you will learn what was going on from her perspective and be able to discuss what (in your own iceberg) was triggered by seeing her chat with that guy.

Undercurrent

A lot of our emotional baggage, beliefs, and values have to do with love relationships. Your iceberg and your partner's iceberg may be filled with issues that can be triggered by the way your relationship is evolving. When these meet in the undercurrent of your difficult talks, it may put extra strain on your ability to stay mindful and not react out of fear or old pain. But when you keep yourself in check here and acknowledge what's going on, it is an excellent opportunity to work through some of your biggest personal challenges. Investigating what is being touched by your partner's behavior is one of the most powerful things you can do for your relationship and for your own development, and talking about them with your partner will deepen your bond considerably.

Synchronicity

Keeping a solid eye on what you want instead of what you fear makes it easier to keep yourself in the mindset of a shared success. Believing there is a way forward that works for both of you, while staying connected to your own needs and being open to theirs (interconnection), will make it possible to recognize potential solutions when they surface.

Exchange

Being aware of how you speak will make all the difference in a romantic relationship. Especially in love relationships, the "always" or "never" trap is close by (for example, "You never do this"), and it's an important one to stay away from. These absolutes will end a positive flow of exchanging perspectives faster than you can speak them, killing off your mindful intention and mindset on the spot. Communicating openly about how their actions make you feel is crucial here.

Reacting from your emotions is obviously not helpful, but neither is offering an "intellectualized," overly rational perspective on what happened. For example, if your partner stood you up on date night, you could speak about how you feared something had happened to her, instead of yelling to directly express the fear or bringing in a bunch of rational arguments to prove that she didn't do the right thing (and altogether dodging your feelings about it). Acknowledge always that there is a difference between how you feel and what your partner meant to do. Separating intention from impact is very helpful when you're confronted with your iceberg: Something inside you has been touched by their actions, but that doesn't mean they meant to hurt you. This allows you to discuss with your partner the root cause of your response, instead of spending time on fighting over an incidental experience.

If You Hurt Them

If you have done something that has hurt your partner, go out of your way to acknowledge their experience, even if it was nowhere near your intention. Acknowledging how they feel is not the same as agreeing with them or taking the blame for something you didn't intend to happen. It does, however, give your partner room to have their experience heard and you the ability to understand why what you did triggered hurt in them.

Mindful Lesson:
The Power of an Apology

Sofía has been struggling at work lately. Her new boss has been criticizing her about basically everything she's been doing. This is taking a huge toll on Sofía: Her work is important to her, and this lack of validation is making her feel pretty low. She's been trying to live up to his expectations by working harder and harder, leaving her little time to really be present at home with her wife and their children. Phillipa, Sofía's wife, knows about the work stress and understands that Sofía is working a little more these days. What Sofía didn't discuss, though, is that she will be working through the upcoming spring break instead of spending time with Phillipa and the kids.

Now that the vacation is nearing, Phillipa wants to start planning the trips they will be taking. When she brings this up, Sofía explodes: "You know I have to do everything I can to improve my position at work. There is no way I can go with you on any of these outings."

Phillipa is hurt: She has been trying to accommodate Sofía for weeks now, and this was something Sofía didn't tell her. Her emotions overtake her, and she bursts into tears.

They decide to step back from the conversation to each take a breath and regroup. After they reconvene, Sofía starts by apologizing: She assumed Phillipa understood that she couldn't be present during their family trips without discussing this with her. Even though she didn't mean to upset Phillipa, she takes responsibility for doing so. She also thanks Phillipa for taking on so much at the house during this difficult time. Phillipa accepts Sofía's apologies. She shares how these past few weeks have been hard on her, too, having to deal with a stressed-out partner and their two children. She realizes Sofía didn't mean to put her under extra pressure, but it happened nonetheless.

After this exchange, they feel connected to each other again. They come up with a plan for Sofía to improve her relationship with her manager and also work on a scaled-down outing schedule for the upcoming vacation.

Some Specific Situations

Following are a couple of common situations you might at one point experience with your partner. For each of these, you'll find a suggestion on how to approach this situation along with an overview of the mindful attitudes that will best serve you when engaging with your significant other about the topic.

Trust Issues

For most people in a committed relationship, trust is one of the most important values. What's tricky is that it's so easy to lose trust, while gaining it takes quite a bit of time. Trust issues can come up when your partner has done something that leads to you losing trust. Or they can come up because of past hurt or your own insecurities. Both of these require open conversations, but of course from different angles.

When your partner has done something that has broken your trust, you will need to discuss what happened, why it happened, and how both of you see your future together. This could well be one of the most difficult conversations you'll ever have. The challenge to stay open and connected will probably be superhard, and the first step is to take some time to sit with your hurt, sending yourself lots of compassion and love. This may sound like a waste of time, but it will help you be at least a little calmer while talking with your partner, which will allow you to listen better and to share more of what you feel, instead of acting out your feelings through yelling or crying.

If you didn't have a previous talk about what you define as infidelity in your relationship, or in other words, what you expect from your partner in return for your trust, you may find out that what you see as a clear breach of trust, your partner sees as a tiny indiscretion. This would lead to a discussion about boundaries after discussing this specific situation to prevent future mishaps. It's very common to need professional support in working through infidelity, so do not hesitate to get a counselor if you find you cannot work through this by yourself.

Mindful Attitudes to Bring In Regarding Infidelity

- Acceptance
- Mindful listening
- Mindful speaking
- Curiosity and sincerity

Another situation around trust arises when you find it hard to give trust to your partner because you have been hurt before or because you struggle with insecurities and low self-esteem. Be mindful of the fact that this is about you, not them, so the conversation will start from you disclosing your challenges in this area and asking for your partner's understanding and support in working through this. You could say something like "When I don't know who you're with and you stay out so late, it triggers my memories about... I know this isn't about you, and still it gets me all worked up. I am working on trusting again. Would you please help me by being very open about whom you spend time with and letting me know when you are staying out late?"

Mindful Attitudes to Bring In Regarding Past Hurts

- Self-disclosure
- Open mind
- Nonjudgment

WHAT IS SELF-DISCLOSURE?

Psychologists Irwin Altman and Dalmas Taylor formulated how interpersonal communication deepens as relationships develop in the social penetration theory. This concept is called "self-disclosure": People gradually share more and more intimate information about themselves. Like an onion being peeled, self-disclosure offers a growing connection and trust with the other person because it invites reciprocal sharing and deep listening.

Household Chores

When you live with your partner, it's important to get clear on who does what around the house right from the start. If you don't, things will eventually sort themselves out but will often lead to the partner with the lower tolerance for chaos and dirt taking care of (many) more tasks around the house. Eventually, this extra work will probably lead to resentment, which is much harder to deal with than the initial challenge of dividing the household chores equally. How do you have this conversation without pointing fingers?

Most people don't really like chores, so it's important to establish a division that works for both of you, which starts by actually taking the time to be fully present for this conversation. Make a list of everything you want and need done in and around the house and divvy the chores up. Be open, complete, and fair. Ideally, you can create a win-win situation if both of you can take on the tasks that you more or less like; for example, your partner hates doing laundry but doesn't have a problem with cleaning the bathroom, which is exactly the other way around for you.

If you got in an unequal rhythm, and you want to bring that up, you can start the conversation by saying something like "I feel I've taken up an unequal part of our household chores. I would like to discuss with you how we can bring back balance." Stay away from finger pointing and accusing your partner of not doing their share. You are an equal part of the problem since you picked up tasks that weren't yours to do, so in order to steer clear of accusations and for you to get what you want, own your part in this.

Be mindful of not wanting a quid pro quo for everything you do around the house, though. It's good to divide things as fairly as possible, but keeping score isn't. It's only normal that at some times, responsibilities may shift a little. That being said, it is important to revisit this topic regularly, because things change and sometimes good habits weaken over time. Times of change—for example, if partners change jobs, children are born, or you move to a large or smaller house—require a conversation to reevaluate your prior agreements.

Mindful Attitudes to Bring In Regarding Chores

- Presence
- Synchronicity
- Win-win

Mindful Lesson:
Letting Go of Assumptions

Alicia and Max have been living together for five years. When they first moved in together, they made a set of agreements dividing the different household chores. This arrangement went well for a couple of years, but lately, as they moved into new jobs with different hours, their routine has been slipping. Alicia now feels she's slowly taken over some of Max's tasks, and she's not happy about that.

She's been thinking about it a lot, and she has discussed it extensively with her friends and her sister. She's come to the conclusion that Max is dodging responsibilities around the house because he feels it should be her who's taking care of the house. Alicia is getting more and more worked up, as this is something she has seen happen with her parents and promised herself wouldn't happen to her.

She has decided to confront Max, and she's thinking through the conversation. What she wants to say is that Max never does his equal part of the household tasks and is apparently trying to push her into being a housewife. Then she catches herself. Approaching Max in that way will almost certainly lead to a hurtful and unhelpful discussion. She realizes she's spun a story about Max's intentions and reasoning behind what's going on, which doesn't have to be true. If she goes into their conversation with this story, he will probably just say that her story isn't true and be mad at her for making assumptions. They've been in fights like that before. This time, she decides to go into this talk with a mindful approach instead.

Letting go of her made-up story about Max's intentions, she shares with Max how his behavior of not doing his part of the chores has led to her picking up the tasks he is not doing (impact). She explains how this has made her feel undervalued and that it has triggered her deeper fear of becoming a housewife like her mom. Max hears her out and realizes that he doesn't feel cornered by her story like he has been in other confrontations. He feels that Alicia is sharing her honest feelings with him, without making him responsible for them. This frees him to fully acknowledge her experience: He says he understands her fears and apologizes for not taking care of his tasks. Alicia feels heard, which allows her to open up to listen to Max's side of the story. After that, they decide to have a look at how they've divided the household chores and discuss if any changes are necessary.

Money Topics

When you're sharing a household with your partner, it's inevitable that you will need to talk about money. Ideally this will not happen when you've already started fighting over it, but right when you begin sharing a household, and then again every time things change. How do you have that dreaded money talk?

When discussing money, it's important to keep in mind that it's a pretty touchy subject and that people have all sorts of different belief systems in place about earning, spending, and saving. It's important to get clear on both of your perspectives on money right from the start and accept where you differ. Maybe you could get the conversation started by suggesting that you capture an overview of both incomes and all joint expenses, after which you both write down how you would like to spend any remaining money (taking into account saving, spending together, and spending on your own) or what to cut back on if necessary. That way, you both have a clear idea of how you see things, and each party has time to consider their feelings and suggestions.

Big problems normally arise when there's secrecy around money, so make it your aim to hide nothing and invite your partner to be completely open, too, by not judging or reacting, primarily when they share information you didn't expect or don't agree with. Take honest inventory of all your spending, and decide together where the money will go. It's often wise to allow each of you your own cash to spend on whatever you please.

Mindful Attitudes to Bring In Regarding Money

- Acceptance
- Open mind
- Honesty
- Mindful speaking
- Mindful listening

When You Disagree on How Much Time You Spend Together

It's perfectly normal to want to spend time together as a couple (and as a family if there are children involved) and to also need time alone. In many relationships, these needs may be more or less the same, but in some they won't be. One partner may need a lot of time alone to feel good, while the other one needs a lot of quality time together to feel loved and appreciated (quality time is one of the languages discussed in *The Five Love Languages*; see the Bibliography at the back of this book). How do you handle this?

The first thing to do is to sit down with your partner to talk about the topic when you aren't having a specific fight about it. This allows both of you to be fully present and open to other perspectives without still feeling stressed from the fight. Take time for both of you to explain your needs, free from judgment or premature conclusions. Listen mindfully, and disclose what you really need and why, bringing up information from your iceberg. Speak about what you need, and realize that both of you can be "right."

People differ greatly in how much alone time they need. It says nothing about your relationship if your partner needs time alone. Do, however, value both "needs" equally and try to find ways forward that do justice to both. It may, for example, be helpful to be very clear about which time is which, and honor that completely. If you are spending time together, make it count and recognize it for what it is. If you or your partner are spending time alone, go all in and do something that will nourish your soul.

Mindful Attitudes to Bring In Regarding How Much Time You Spend Together

- Presence
- Self-disclosure
- Synchronicity
- And Stance and win-win mentality

Intimacy and Sex

Intimacy and sex may not be the easiest topics to discuss, but you have to find the courage to talk about them. Remember, your partner cannot read your mind. How do you raise such a personal subject, one that for quite a lot of people brings up self-consciousness or even shame?

Begin by acknowledging that a conversation is in order, and share that with your partner. Avoid doing this in your bedroom or after you just had sex. It's helpful to have this talk on neutral ground. When you're having the conversation, focus on your needs and use your curiosity to determine the needs of your partner. Summarize what you hear, focusing on the values and needs you share, to create more common ground. Intimacy and sexuality are topics that can bring both of you together, so focus on that.

Make sure you avoid "never" and "always" in this talk, and if your partner uses them, talk about that first. Struggling against blockers like that will make it much harder to connect. You may want to start the conversation by saying something like "I would love to have more opportunity to really connect with you physically," or "I love the closeness of having sex with you." This way you're slowly moving in, focusing on your connection with your partner, instead of confronting your partner with something harsh like "Our sex life is deteriorating" or "We do not make love often enough."

By sharing something about your needs, and combining that with curiosity about what your partner wants, you immediately bring in the golden partnership, and through that the right mindset to have this conversation in connection.

Mindful Attitudes to Bring In Regarding Your Sex Life

- Nonjudgment
- Open mind
- Acceptance
- Self-disclosure
- Sincerity and curiosity

Discussing Your Roles and Values As Parents

The moment you and your partner become parents, you step into new roles that will have an effect on the dynamics between the two of you. Also, you'll need a new shared perspective on your values and both of your roles as parents. This conversation will continue to be on the table for the years to come, as children and their needs change regularly. How can you talk about these new roles, upcoming challenges, and your parenting styles?

First, it's important to accept that, even though you may have a lot in common, it's not strange if you and your partner have different ideas about raising your child. Topics like how to help your baby sleep, how much screen time is okay for your preschooler, or how to handle your teenager's need for independence are difficult, and finding a shared approach is definitely not always easy. However, knowing and accepting each other's viewpoint and perspective on the most ideal parenting style is a great start.

It may be tempting to prepare yourself for every potential challenge with your child by setting strict rules together and making agreements on how to handle any possible case. This isn't helpful for three reasons:

1. You will not encounter every problem in this book.

2. When things actually happen, there are always different aspects to take into account than you thought of when it was a hypothetical situation.

3. When you discuss things that are relevant right now by using PAUSE, synchronicity can help you come up with a solution that you may have never considered in advance.

What will really help is when you know how your partner wants to be as a parent. People's beliefs, values, and ideas about good parenting are often based on their own experiences as a child. It helps if you are both able to share the parts of your iceberg that relate to parenting. This requires disclosure and mindful listening.

Knowing each other's goals in parenting will also make it easier to have each other's backs and offer your children a united front even though you may not always agree 100 percent. You want to sustain an open line of communication about each partner's perspective on the children and on how to handle the challenges that come with being a parent.

A fun way to start this open line of communication is to make a list of your shared values as a family. Think of five to ten values and ideals you want to live by together (for example, talking instead of yelling, not calling each other names, and not going to bed angry). Your family values can be evaluated regularly (once a year, for example), and as your children get a little older they can contribute, which creates buy-in.

Mindful Attitudes to Bring In Regarding Parenting

- Acceptance and nonjudgment
- Presence
- Synchronicity
- Curiosity and mindful listening
- Self-disclosure

PAUSE IN ACTION: WHAT DO YOU WANT FOR YOURSELF?

After reading these common challenges people face with their partners, you may have found areas where there's room for improvement in your own relationship. Before plunging in and discussing everything at once, take a bit of time to digest and explore what you want out of your relationship. It's really healthy to regularly assess if you're still on track together, and even though figuring that out will eventually involve an open conversation, it is also necessary to first know how you feel.

Carve out some alone time and pick a spot where you can be comfortable for at least an hour or so. Bring a pen and paper. Center yourself using abdominal breathing or doing a (guided) meditation (see the Online Resources section at the back of this book). Set the intention to uncover your true feelings, and freewrite your answers to the following questions, meaning you just write without judging or editing it. The goal is to uncover some of your deeper feelings and needs.

Answer each of these questions:

1. What are the values you want to live your life by?
2. What is most important to you in a relationship?
3. Which of these values and things you find important are currently in your life?
4. Which aren't?

Imagine you are at the end of your long, fruitful life:

1. What do you want to see when you look back?
2. What gave you the most rewards in your relationships?
3. What do you truly want for yourself in a relationship?

After answering these questions, go over the answers and consider the impact of what you wrote down. Looking at your relationship with this sense of perspective, what topics are most important to discuss with your partner? Write down the key points to bring into the conversation with your partner, but leave room for being present and seeing what happens in the talk.

CHAPTER SUMMARY

The following are takeaways, action steps, and reminders to support you in taking on the difficult conversations with your love, bringing both of you closer together.

● Challenging situations with your partner are extra hard because you may be expecting a little too much of this one individual.

● It's helpful to discern where your partner's behavior is causing unnecessary strain while at the same time being aware of your own unhealed pain surfacing. By taking ownership of the latter, it's much easier to discuss how your partner can support you instead of making things worse.

● The PAUSE approach supports you in the hard talks with your partner by reminding you to make time to really be present with them and the topic you're discussing. Be aware of the stories you may be running in your head and literally call them out.

● Especially in your love relationship, it's helpful to gradually disclose more and more about your personal iceberg. The more your partner knows about your true feelings, needs, beliefs, and past experiences, the easier it will be to have positive and supportive conversations. If you do not know these things about each other, this unexpressed stuff will be interfering in the undercurrent of your conversation, making it much harder to find win-win solutions.

CHAPTER 9
USING THE PAUSE
APPROACH WITH FAMILY

"The informality of family life is a blessed
condition that allows us all to become
our best while looking our worst."

Marge Kennedy

Ideally, the members of your family know you very well, appreciate you for who you are, and support you throughout all the different stages of your life. But what if this isn't the case?

If challenges arise between family members, things become complicated pretty fast. Because of how well your family knows you, misunderstandings and disagreements hurt deeply. You might say that with family, there's vulnerability ingrained in the relationship. You didn't get to gradually disclose information about yourself; it's all out in the open because your family members have known you your entire life (and vice versa, of course). Because they know your true self, their opinions touch you on a deeper level. In this chapter, you will learn how the PAUSE approach can support you in disputes with your family members. A couple of common situations will illustrate the use of the approach in real life. First, let's explore in more detail what makes the disputes with family members specifically challenging.

The Challenges of Difficult Conversations with Family Members

You've probably heard it before: You can't choose your family! And while some members of your (extended) family might be your closest friends and confidants, others might not be. Some of them have known you since you were a child, but they may not see that much of you these days, so their understanding of you is concentrated on your childhood years. Family is a highly complicated situation that can lead to unconditional love—and to intense arguments and deep-seated disputes.

Family Influences Who You Are

Your relationships with various family members—especially your parents and siblings—have a tremendous influence on who you are and who you will become. Through both genetics and experiences, your family and close relatives have a big influence on how you develop in life. They affect many things, from your preferred diet to your personal values and beliefs about the world. Your parents have shaped you in how they taught you, but through them, your grandparents and earlier ancestors have added to the mix too. Both genetics and behavior are passed on through the generations, leading to a deeply ingrained family system.

Even when you do not get along with some of them, they will still (sometimes negatively) influence your beliefs about yourself and ideas about the world. Take, as a straightforward example, your aunt who shares your auburn hair, or your grandfather, who, like you, puts on weight from just looking at pasta. On a personality level, imagine a cousin you find a little annoying, as she meddles in other people's business so readily, but if you're completely honest, you must admit you have a bit of that too. Or consider your grandmother's special saying that you keep hearing in the back of your mind, even now that she's passed away.

To understand yourself, you will have to make an effort to identify and understand your family dynamics. In communicating with your family, this shared history and these long-standing patterns can provide helpful information, but they can also make things harder. It is so easy to fall into the same unhelpful patterns over and over again if you do not approach these kinds of talks with awareness.

Managing Decades of History

Your family relations can easily last for decades. This history can create a focus on the past and how things have "always" been. Yet at various points in your life, your relationships with your family members will have to evolve. An easy example is the relationship between a child and parents—when the child grows older, their relationship will adapt to fit the new dynamics: from baby to child, to teenager, to young adult, to adult. Or consider how the relationships with your siblings evolve after you no longer live in the same house. Or think about the changes in the relationship between you and your grandparents who used to live on the same block your entire childhood and who have now moved into a nursing home in another state. With every step, you will somehow need to renegotiate how to relate.

Problems Between Two Relatives Affect the Group

Another challenge within families arises because troubles between two members will often affect the group as a whole. Imagine that you've had a fight with your dad that isn't fully resolved, so the aftereffects are still lingering. Your mom and brother notice that something is going on between the two of you. Your mom has a talk with your dad about what is going on. Maybe they have words about the way your father has been handling the situation so far. Your younger brother may be annoyed by all the commotion and adds to the fire by bringing up how your father normally always agrees with you, so the reason for your current fight must be a serious one. This illustrates how even a simple fight can upset an entire family system. Imagine the further impact of more significant troubles or a large family unit.

How the Mindful Approach Will Support You

The undercurrent is a force for good in family relations. It's really easy to make assumptions about and expect certain behavior from the people you've known so long and so well, but those assumptions and expectations may be clouding your judgment as to who they really are now. Using PAUSE will help you bring out unspoken information from the undercurrent so you will be able to discuss what really matters in the current moment.

Presence

In your difficult situations with members of your family, it's easy to get sidetracked by the patterns you are in together. Your mom always responds like this, so it's not necessary to really listen to her this time around. But if you don't really listen today, you will never hear anything new. Do not let your previous experiences dictate your reaction; instead, be with the person fully now and explore if there's a new possible way to respond.

Your personal presence is important too. Any preset expectations will influence how you approach the conversation. If your expectations are negatively colored, the energy you bring with you will be accordingly negative. Allow yourself to approach them differently this time—otherwise, you will just get what you've always gotten.

Acceptance

It's important to accept family members and situations as they are and to be prepared to find a positive way to work on making connections better. Refrain from saying things like "Aunt Lucy just is that way; you'd better accept that she will always be meddling in your private business." This is not the type of acceptance that mindfulness incorporates. Instead, it means that you accept your aunt and the situation as they are now but also work toward a new way of interaction that respects both needs. In the example of Aunt Lucy, she has a habit of meddling, which is the situation right now. However, you find that intrusive, so you enter into a sincere conversation to explain how her meddling affects you and to come to a way forward that respects your need to make your own decisions and her (underlying) need to be part of your life. For example, you may agree to post regular updates in the family group app, and she may agree to refrain from commenting about the best way to handle whatever is going on for you. By accepting what is true now, you stop fighting it, and when you stop fighting, you will be open to explore how to grow. It's important to appreciate the past without holding on to it and to be open to see your loved ones with beginner's eyes.

Undercurrent

The deeper layers of your personality are inherently wrapped up in your family members. Both you and your family members evolve over time, obviously, but in longer relationships, it's so easy to forget that and continue to see the other person as they were years ago. By disclosing elements from your iceberg, you will create a supportive atmosphere of openheartedness. You may even want to support your family members who do not know about the undercurrent by tapping into it through them and helping them bring out what's going on for them on a deeper level. For example, you could say something like "Tio, I feel how much you want to connect with my mom, but it seems like you're on different wavelengths. Maybe it will help to tell her you've missed her a lot?"

In family relationships, boundaries may be a more common topic than in other types of relations. Ideally, boundaries are just openly discussed, but if they aren't, you will probably be able to pick them up from the undercurrent. If you do, be respectful of them. Make them explicit: "I sense you're setting a boundary here; is that correct?" And affirm them while also being honest about your needs.

Synchronicity

When you embrace an open mind and allow the undercurrent to work for you, you can expect pleasant surprises. Assuming you and your family member basically have a healthy and positive relationship, the underlying connection and love will support you throughout the harder moments and allow solutions to arise.

Exchange

In discussing your challenges with your relatives, be extra mindful of the way you speak. Your tone of voice says a lot about your underlying beliefs, and often your relatives know you so well that they are very sensitive to your tone, volume, word choice, and body language. Embracing your family members as they are while also knowing your relationship has evolved will help you stay out of the "we have been through this a thousand times" tone or the "I am your father, so I know what is right for you" tone. Be completely respectful of their sovereign right to make their own choices while also being open about your perspective and your wishes (when relevant).

REAL-TIME ISSUES

Be extra mindful of the possibility that the reason why you are having the conversation may play itself out in the conversation. If you notice irritation in yourself or your relative, look at how you're both behaving in the moment. It's really powerful to be able to use what is happening now as an illustration of what is happening in the broader perspective.

Mindful Lesson:
Exploring Family Dynamics

Forty-year-old Allison is having dinner with her father, Ronald. They have talked about many things, and the atmosphere is friendly and open. The conversation turns to Mary's plans for a career change. She has been working for an international company for many years, but she has recently decided to take a bold leap: She is quitting her job to pursue an exciting but uncertain new opportunity as an entrepreneur. She's aware that this will probably mean she won't be earning anywhere near the amount she was before, but she has saved more than enough money to make it through at least a couple of years with little income.

Ronald is surprised, to say the least. He's always been proud of Allison for making it in the corporate world, and this is not what he had hoped for his child. He tries to be supportive, though. He says, "That's great news, honey. I am very excited for you." He then changes the subject to Allison's brother, who just got a promotion at his job.

While Allison listens to her father, she feels her emotions rising. Her father's words don't mean anything to her, as she picks up on his underlying surprise and judgment, which brings up old pain of not being supported by her father in earlier choices she made. He always disapproved of her decisions, and it's no different now, even though she's forty. The fact that he isn't honest about it hurts her even more. As she feels herself drawing away from him more and more, she catches herself. What is she doing? She wants her relationship with her father to become better, and here she is, falling back into their old pattern. Instead of sulking about the opinions she senses, she decides to bring them out.

"Dad, I'm sorry to interrupt, but can we circle back to my plans for a minute? I hear you are trying to support me, but I am also sensing that you might feel unsure about it. Can we talk about what you are really thinking about my decision?"

Ronald is taken aback, but he regroups quickly and says, "Allison, we have been in so many fights about my thoughts about your decisions—I don't want that anymore. Also, you're a grown-up now; who am I to have opinions about your life?"

"You are my father," says Allison, "and your opinion matters to me. I'd rather openly talk about why we have different opinions than pretend to be in agreement."

"I see your point," says Ronald, and he starts explaining that, because he grew up having to be very conscious about money, he doesn't want that for his children. That is something Allison hadn't realized, and before they know it, they are exploring the underlying beliefs and values that bring forth their different perspectives on entrepreneurship.

Some Specific Situations

Following are a couple of situations you may recognize from interacting with your family. For each of these, you'll find a suggestion on how to approach the situation and an overview of the mindful attitudes that will best serve you when engaging with your relatives.

When You Disagree with a Relative about a Personal Situation

Even your closest family members will not always support the choices you make about your personal life. Whether the issue at hand is religion, a career, politics, or your choice of life partner, it will be impossible to always agree with everyone. Disagreement in itself isn't necessarily a bad thing, as long as you are able to openly speak about it and respect each other's points of view. How do you discuss these very personal and quite often emotionally charged topics without harming the relationship?

Although it will probably be difficult, try to stay away from overpreparing when you see a conversation like this coming. If you start guessing what they will say and then what you will say in return, you will be stuck in the old patterns and won't be able to see what is actually happening or what the potential is in the conversation. Of course, it is good to go over your "why," the reasons behind your perspective, before you get into it, but beyond that, allow for a truly open conversation, where synchronicities may lead you in a different direction than you ever could have imagined.

In discussing personal topics, always be prepared to handle strong emotions. As you learned in Chapter 4, emotions are unexpressed feelings boiling up, so they're to be expected in a personal conversation like this and not something to be scared of. Use what you sense in the undercurrent to bring out what the other person may not be consciously aware of yet, and of course what is happening with you.

Make it a priority to create interconnection and bring in the And Stance. If you notice the other person is still thinking in "either/or" terms, kindly explain how you can both be right at the same time, especially in personal topics. For example, if you and your brother disagree on the best way to spend your shared vacation, and he keeps insisting that you should come to an agreement as to which option is the best one (perhaps going to the mountains or the beach), you can explain that each person's preference is completely valid and suggest that, instead of fighting about it, you'd rather spend time searching for a destination that offers both.

Mindful Attitudes to Bring In Regarding Personal Choices

- Allow the conversation to unfold in the moment (instead of overpreparing)
- Undercurrent
- Interconnection
- And Stance

Boundary Issues

Maybe your child doesn't want you to call every day to check in, or maybe your mother is no longer willing to do your laundry now that you have your own apartment: It's all part of the normal evolution of relationships. Boundaries are not easy to tackle, but taking the time to establish them will make life easier going forward.

First know this: Setting boundaries is a highly normal and necessary part of the transition into adult life. So if, for example, your child needs you to take a step back, know that it doesn't mean you can no longer have a meaningful relationship with them. If it's the other way around, and your parents tell you they will no longer take care of your every need, this is part of growing up. It's okay.

The second step is to get really clear on what is and what isn't okay for you. You may not know immediately, so take some time to figure this out for yourself before you engage in the conversation. Also consider where you do want to have interaction (for example, when you do value someone's opinions and suggestions or when you do want your niece to know that she can call you in an emergency).

When you have the conversation, approach the topic by expressing your needs and the underlying reasons for them. Make sure your requests don't seem to be punishment or coming out of resentment or anger. Talking about boundaries is also an important opportunity to express gratitude for your relationship. Be kind. This topic may be pretty intense for either one of you, so be prepared for emotions to rise. Continue to stay present, even if there's pushback. There is no need to alter your position, but allow the other person time to get used to your new boundaries.

Mindful Attitudes to Bring In Regarding Boundaries

- Personal check-in
- Kindness and gratitude
- Mindful speaking
- Presence

When You Don't Get Along with a Sibling

It's certainly not uncommon for people to have both their best and their most painful relationships with their siblings. One reason why sibling relations can be hard to improve is that your subconscious mind doesn't understand the passing of time. When your sibling does something that upsets you, you are immediately transported back to childhood and your automatic reaction is often remembering the family role you had as a kid. Say, for example, your older brother always teased you about spending all your time playing with dolls, which made you feel inferior and belittled at the time. Nowadays, you will probably experience those same feelings when your brother teasingly comments on your intense interest in how people interact, even though this happens decades later.

Since you likely grew up in the same house, lived with the same people, and dealt with the same values and rules, you and your siblings might have similar ways of handling difficult situations. You need only one person to start an open, mindful conversation, but if neither one of you was taught how to do that, your discussions may not have been mindful thus far. On the other hand, if you change your behavior, the entire family system can shift as well.

When you decide to start a conversation about the problems you're having together, it's helpful to acknowledge how hard it is to stay out of your family roles by making that part of the conversation. It can be helpful to also disclose how you felt in relation to your sibling growing up. Maybe there was rivalry, jealousy, or competition for parental love and attention involved. By disclosing some of your experiences, you bring in openness and vulnerability, inviting your sibling to also share more.

Sincerely speaking about why you want your relationship with your sibling to improve may serve as a heartful reminder to yourself and as an inspiration to your sibling. Be curious about their needs: How do they see your relationship improving? Trust that a win-win situation is possible, even though it may look completely different from what you thought it would be. If something concrete has happened that caused a fallout (instead of your relationship slowly deteriorating), be open to see that you can both be right. Always be open to apologizing sincerely if that is what is called for.

Mindful Attitudes to Bring In Regarding Siblings

- Self-disclosure
- Sincerity
- Curiosity
- And Stance
- If appropriate: apologize

Mindful Lesson:
How to Handle Disconnect

Carter and Matt are brothers. They grew up together and lived in the same house until Carter moved out to go to college. As kids, they had a reasonably good relationship, often shooting hoops in front of their house or playing soccer together.

In their house, they didn't talk about feelings much. Their mom sometimes complained a little, but she always put her feelings aside. As adults, Carter and Matt got a little more comfortable sharing their feelings with their respective romantic partners, but with each other, they didn't ever really open up.

Over time, their relationship slowly deteriorated. They started seeing each other less and less for no particular reason; they just didn't make time for it. Carter would like to see this change, and he sets up a face-to-face meeting with Matt to talk about this. In the days before their meeting, Carter is constantly thinking about how he could approach this. He knows he will need to go a little deeper to explain why he wants things to change between them. He decides to call his friend Ethan, who is always very good at talking about feelings. Ethan laughs when Carter asks him how he might explain to Matt why he wants them to be closer because he doesn't know how. "More than anything, talking about what you are feeling requires practice. Man, do you know how many times I sat through our family meetings as a kid?" Ethan says. "But I can give you a few pointers: Be sincere and tell Matt what you want. You know, it's quite beautiful, actually—the conversation you are going to have is an example of how you want things to be from now on, right?"

That is right, Carter realizes. The next day when he meets Matt, that sentiment is what he starts with: "I have been postponing this talk because I find it really hard to talk about what I feel for you, but I realized that what I was running away from was exactly what I also wanted for us: to be closer and more connected and to be able to share what is really going on with us." Matt didn't see this coming, but he has been thinking along the same lines for a while. He'd even discussed it with his wife a few weeks back. Before they know it, they are having a great time sharing stories of how their limited experience in talking about feelings led to struggle when they first started dating. From there, they hash out a plan to get together more regularly.

When Your Teen Pushes Your Buttons

If you're a parent of a teenager, you are probably familiar with the eye rolls, the shrugging, the withdrawal, and the pushing your buttons. Teenagers are still technically children, but they are really great at knowing exactly how to trigger you, making it so hard not to react from a place of pain. Staying out of tunnel vision and keeping a calm mind may sound good in theory, but how do you do that in real life?

Here are a couple of things to remind yourself of regularly so they will be ingrained when things get hard:

- This is a normal phase.
- This phase is hard on them too.
- They are not yet an adult, but you are.

You know that fighting back when they act a certain way is very counterproductive. The mindful approach can be a lifesaver here.

Following PAUSE is the best way to go. Begin by taking a few deep breaths, re-centering yourself. Try at all costs not to take the bait. Breathe and just be present with them. You don't have anything to solve or to prove right now. You are the parent; they are the child. They are struggling, but there is no reason to join them in that struggle. Accept your situation as it is right now, and explore the undercurrent via a personal check-in: Are they crossing any real boundaries? Meanness doesn't have to be tolerated (but don't respond right now). You can help bring the emotions out by naming what you pick up in the undercurrent: Is it anger, fear, frustration? Listen deeply to what comes up and allow the emotion to play itself out while practicing mindful awareness and just being present with what is, without judgment of yourself or your child.

Because you are not adding to the fire, after a while your teen will settle down, and then you can start the conversation. If things get heated again, tell them you are postponing talking until later when they have cooled down. This talk is about why they got so emotional. You can offer understanding, and you may ask if they want some tips if the frustration was aimed at other people. This is also when you circle back to any meanness or intolerable behavior. The most important takeaway here is to pause so you can stop yourself from engaging.

Mindful Attitudes to Bring In Regarding Teenagers

- Deep breathing
- Personal check-in
- Acceptance
- Undercurrent
- Mindful listening

TAKING CARE OF YOURSELF

After a discussion with a teenager, it's time to recuperate and regroup. Whether you prefer doing a metta meditation, going on a walk, playing some sports, writing in your journal, or taking a shower to wash it off, take some time for yourself. Be mindful of yourself now. Acknowledge that this wasn't easy, and it wasn't fun. Maybe you managed to stay calm, or maybe you didn't this time, but either way, you've learned something. Be appreciative of the progress you made since the last incident.

Self-care is important, because you can only be a good parent if you take care of yourself. This sets an example for your children as well: This is how you can also deal with stress; there's no need to yell, but do acknowledge it and allow yourself to feel it.

When You Want to Blend Two Families

Combining two family systems after finding a new partner is common, but that doesn't mean it is simple. Added to the challenges any marriage faces, when bringing together children from previous relations in one household you are confronted with an entire arsenal of special "blended family problems." How can you approach this in a mindful way?

First, accept that this may not be simple and that it will take more time than you expect. In the beginning, things may feel as if you're simply two families who share a house. That's okay. Include the children in discussing values and house rules in an age-appropriate way so they have a say in what happens to them.

If they are upset about the new formation, listen to them mindfully. Perhaps they are grieving over the old family system or having trouble settling in with the new one. Sibling rivalry may have a new definition now that there are more siblings involved, and maybe one or more kids feels they get too little attention. These challenges are part of the process. If possible, have these talks together with your partner, unless this worsens the anxiety in the child. Respond mindfully, acknowledging the struggles and appreciating everyone's efforts to make it work (even if you don't really have any proof of that yet).

Mindful Attitudes to Bring In Regarding Blended Families

- Acceptance
- Mindful listening
- Mindful speaking

CHAPTER SUMMARY

The following are takeaways, action steps, and reminders to support you in having the conversations that matter with your relatives.

● Difficult conversations with your family are extra challenging because you didn't get to choose your family members, and you have a long history with them. Because of deeply ingrained family systems, you may easily find yourself falling into old patterns.

● Tapping into the undercurrent is how to tackle family conflicts. A lot of your iceberg is formed in the interaction with your family, and the subconscious brain doesn't distinguish between past and present, so you can easily get sucked back into old habits and patterns. By tapping into what is going on below the waterline, both for yourself and your relative, you will be able to bring out that old stuff and use it as valuable information for the conversation you're having now. Unearthing these underlying issues will create opportunities such as new understanding, new solutions, and new connection.

● Accepting each other's boundaries may be the biggest overall challenge in family relations. In no other bond is it so hard to walk the line between healthy engagement and unasked-for interference. The PAUSE approach supports you in this by helping you be kind and thoughtful in bringing up this issue (if you are being meddled with) and helping you to sense when you go too far and have an open, respectful conversation about it (if you are the meddler).

CHAPTER 10
USING THE PAUSE APPROACH WITH FRIENDS

"Lots of people want to ride with you in the limo, but what you want is someone who will take the bus with you when the limo breaks down."

Oprah Winfrey

Maintaining good friendships in adulthood is really important for overall well-being. Your friends are the people you choose to be around, and they can play a vital role in how you handle both the good and the sad things in life. Yet maintaining healthy, open, and truly supportive relationships with your friends can be a source of worry too. You may have experienced how over time, friendships lose their common basis, because one of you progresses in life or because you spend less time together because of new priorities.

This chapter will go into some of the most common themes and challenges you may face when interacting with your friends, and how the approaches you've learned throughout Parts 1 and 2 of this book will support you in handling them in a positive, thoughtful way. First let's explore what facets are specific to difficult situations with friends.

The Challenges of Difficult Conversations with Friends

Many people have varying friendships over time, changing friends when they change jobs or move to another place. Like all relationships, friendships need maintenance to stay up to date, especially when life's circumstances change.

You Do Choose Your Friends

Unlike the relationships you have with your family members, you can freely choose your friends. Friendships also face a lot of transition because they are often made in certain situations (schools, workplaces, and so on), and those situations often change. Because you evolved, the friendship also evolved. Or maybe it didn't, but it should have. This in itself may cause difficult situations, which in turn may lead to difficult conversations. How do you work through these challenges, including knowing when it's worthwhile to solve them and when it's time to let go of the people you have outgrown?

High Expectations

Another challenge in adult friendships is that people tend to have pretty high expectations of their friends: They should know you really well; be there when you need them; and be selfless and interested in your life, while at the same time sharing openly about their own lives too.

FRIENDSHIPS MAY PROLONG LIFE

According to "The Health Benefits of Friendship," a blog post by psychotherapist Joseph Burgo, PhD, supportive friends help you "buffer" the harmful effects stress has on you, because they allow you to vent and give you support. Another theory is that by belonging to a social network, you get inspired to take better care of yourself by the healthy friends in the group. Being healthy also improves your self-esteem.

When you spend a lot of time together, those expectations may be okay. But when one or both of you have a demanding job or a family to look after, you may not see each other as often as you used to. And when that happens, those high expectations might become too high for a friend to live up to. Your assumptions of your friendship may no longer be realistic, which can lead to misunderstandings, annoyances, and irritations. These things can very easily spin out of control when not handled promptly, which may be even more of a challenge if you don't see each other that often.

Less Urgent

For some people, their friendships are the most important thing in the world, but for others, that's not true. Many adults have other relationships they find more important, like with their partner, children, and immediate family. Sometimes, friendships become less urgent as life progresses. The challenge in this scenario is twofold:

1. Your friend may experience things differently, and this might cause you to have different ideas about the importance of your friendship.

2. The fact that friendship may not be as valuable as, for example, the relationship with your partner, it might keep you from going through the trouble of resolving the problems you run into, which may lead to a rift between you.

Here's a positive way to look at friendships that are less urgent: The fact that there may be less pressure on the relationship offers you a safe opportunity to practice speaking up.

Striking a Balance Between Support and Addressing the Issues

At one point you may find yourself in a situation where your friend makes decisions that you feel aren't healthy for them, like staying in a relationship that doesn't make them happy, pursuing a career that doesn't bring out the best in them, or not taking care of themselves physically (as with, for example, alcohol or substance abuse).

In these type of situations, striking a balance between being there for them and giving them constructive feedback becomes a real challenge. You want to show that you support them, that you are on their side, and that you can see things through their eyes. On the other hand, you will most likely also want to help them get out of this harmful situation. Finding the right balance between these two isn't easy, and it may take a good deal of consideration and a careful approach that spreads out over time.

How the Mindful Approach Will Support You

In friendships, it's really easy to let previous experiences, expectations, and assumptions run the show. The challenge is to not allow that to happen. Your use of the PAUSE approach will support that.

Presence

Because you don't see most of your friends every day, all day, quite often your relationships lean heavily on how things used to be. The past might be an important factor in how you see them: they are such an important friend because they were there for you back when you went through that nasty breakup; they are your best friend because you two spent so much time together in college.

But is that still true now? Being present will support you in assessing what is in fact relevant today.

Acceptance

To truly appreciate the value of the friendship today, it's so important to bring in acceptance and concepts like beginner's mind and nonjudgment when you feel challenged by your friends. If something happens, putting your mind to rest by thinking that "things will return to normal" or that "it isn't such a big deal" won't do you much good. See your friend and the situation as they are right now.

When you accept that it's necessary to bring something up verbally, you will prevent issues from lingering until the next time you see your friend. By engaging quickly, you can keep things in proportion, making it easier to work through them. Always check what you are thinking about a situation, using curiosity instead of going into assumptions.

Undercurrent

Friendships are a great place to practice tapping into the undercurrent and bringing up the things you sense are going on. Friendships are often a safe space to uncover things about yourself and speak about what you find is going on beyond the literal topic of conversation.

Even though you may have known each other for years, continue to be curious about what is really going on with your friend by practicing mindful listening. This technique can even deepen your bond when you thought you'd grown apart.

Synchronicity

Maybe your love and appreciation for your friend will make it easier to remember to be patient, generous, and grateful and to embrace a win-win approach. When things are heating up, remember interconnection and how your friend, like you, is probably just trying to make sure they are happy, feel safe, and avoid suffering. Trust that in the moment, potential solutions will come up and that you will recognize them when they do.

Exchange

However straightforward and right it may seem to blame your friend for what is wrong between you, it's important to realize that you are still the co-owner of the situation—even when they did something that has upset you. Avoid the drama triangle and embrace the skills you learned in Chapter 6 to speak in a mindful and sincere way, influencing the course the conversation will take.

Some Specific Situations

Following are a couple of common situations you might at one point experience with your friends. For each of these, you'll find a suggestion on how to approach this situation and an overview of the mindful attitudes that will best serve you when engaging with your friends about the topic.

When Friends Break Promises or Cancel Dates

Some people make a habit of canceling or changing plans at the last minute—for example, maybe a friend bailed on your birthday party. How can you bring this up without harming the friendship?

The most crucial thing to remember here is the importance of raising the subject and not letting it linger because you "don't want to be
a pest" or "they probably have a good reason." They probably do have
a good reason, and it is important to hear it from them and not make
it up yourself. Also, here it's important to remember that their reasons
matter and your feelings matter just as much. How you felt when your
friend didn't show up or canceled your plan is just as important as
their reasons for doing it. They deserve to know that they hurt you.

Engage with a constructive intention and mindset and with loads
of curiosity and sincerity, and stay open to hear their story. You could
use a sentence like this to start the conversation: "I really appreciate
everything you are going through/how busy you are/etc., but when
you didn't show up as promised, I felt sad and let down. I really needed you in that moment. Could you explain what made you decide not
to be there?"

Mindful Attitudes to Bring In Regarding Broken Promises

- And Stance
- Mindful listening
- Interconnection
- Golden partnership: curiosity and sincerity

Mindful Lesson:
Understanding a Friend's Choices

Chris is marrying his girlfriend, Lisa. His college friend Andrew has been invited, but after an initial acceptance, Andrew cancels his attendance a day before the wedding. Chris is surprised and hurt, especially since Andrew didn't
call him personally but just sent a message to the wedding planner listed on
his wedding website.

In the weeks after the wedding, Chris wonders aloud with Lisa about
Andrew's cancellation. What could have been going on? The last time they saw

each other they seemed to be in such different places: While Chris was sharing about the preparation for the wedding, Andrew had just split up with his boyfriend and was considering quitting his job to travel. Chris wonders if his absence has to do with Andrew not feeling up to the wedding vibe since he's in such a different place himself.

Finally, after another long talk full of assumptions, Lisa suggests that Chris meet with Andrew to tell him how he feels and ask him what happened. Even though Chris feels nervous about it, and the reasons not to do it are running through his mind, he does meet up with Andrew. After a little bit of small talk, he brings up the question that's on this mind: "Andrew, I have been wondering what made you cancel your attendance to my wedding. What happened?"

Andrew seems to hesitate, then takes a deep breath and says: "I know, that was probably a bad call, but I really couldn't get myself to come to your wedding and celebrate while I am still struggling with my breakup with Tom. I chose to honor my own feelings."

Chris nods. He understands, but he is also upset: There was no emergency to make missing the wedding acceptable; Andrew just didn't want to come. Instead of shaming Andrew, though, he embraces a mindful mindset: Andrew didn't do this to hurt him or because he doesn't appreciate him as a friend, but because he was trying to care for his own needs. He decides to uncover a bit more of his feelings about this: "I really appreciate what you're going through with Tom, but you missing my wedding without an explanation made me question our friendship. I really needed you in that moment."

Andrew picks up on Chris's constructive approach: "I am so very sorry I couldn't be there for you. Is there a way I can make it up to you?"

When Friends Make Poor Life Choices

Maybe you have a friend who continues to attract the kind of boy-friends who take advantage of her, maybe one of your friends is abusing alcohol, or maybe a friend is spending more money than is wise. How can you bring up your opinion about their life choices without harming your friendship?

First of all, before you say anything, remember that since it is their life, you should tread carefully. On the other hand, since they are your friend, you cannot let them do things that seem to be causing them pain or harm without making an effort to support them in making another choice. The first time you bring it up, you can approach it rather casually, focusing on offering support. For example, you could say, "I have noticed you have been drinking quite a lot lately. Are you stressed out about something? I just wanted to see if there is anything I can do to support you."

It is smart to make this first attempt as soon as it becomes an issue. This way, you haven't been struggling with it for too long, which would make it hard to keep your opinions and judgment under control.

If your friend doesn't want help and/or things do not change, you need to consider how this situation is affecting your relationship and your life. Do you still want to be friends with them if they keep up this behavior? You probably need to bring it up again, and this time you'll need to be firmer and say, "You haven't made any real changes since we last spoke, and I notice that your habits are influencing our friendship/my life/etc. How do you see this?" Then continue with something like "This needs to change if you want us to stay friends. Is there anything you need to change this habit?"

Depending on the impact their behavior has on your relationship, there may be a point where you will need to end the friendship formally. If you decide on that, focus the "breakup" on your needs, as in "I have found that I cannot continue to support you, and because that is what friends are for, I cannot be your friend right now." As in all conversations where you need to break bad news, it's much easier if there is a clear trail of previous talks that led up to your decision.

Mindful Attitudes to Bring In Regarding Friends Making Poor Choices

- Acceptance
- Open mind
- Mindful speaking
- Mindful listening

Mindful Lesson: Practicing Acceptance

Jada and Heather have been friends for years. They are now in their thirties, and their friendship is still solid. Even though they no longer live in the same city, they make time to see each other regularly. Lately, their friendship has been under some pressure. Heather's husband is in a very stressful job, which puts a lot of pressure on him. He apparently doesn't deal with that well, and he takes his stress out on Heather and their kids. He hasn't been violent, but his verbal and emotional abuse is painful and puts Heather in an awful position. She used to love her husband very much, and she doesn't want her boys to grow up in a broken family. On the other hand, the pressure is huge, and she feels she's not setting a good example for her children by staying in this horrible situation. Also, she realizes she is putting extra strain on the situation by pressuring her husband to find help and pointing out how bad his behavior is for their children.

She shares what's going on with Jada. At first Jada is supersupportive: She validates Heather's ideas and opinions fully. She's understanding of her perspective on things, and she brainstorms ideas of Heather leaving. But in the following months, nothing really changes. And Jada finds herself holding back a little in agreeing with what Heather is telling her. She realizes Heather isn't taking any concrete steps and keeps herself in a situation that doesn't seem to be changing at all. Heather seems to get more and more depressed about the situation, and her energy starts to affect Jada, leaving her to feel tired and drained after spending time with Heather.

Jada realizes she has to change her approach, and she decides to call out Heather's passiveness. When they next meet she brings up the subject; she's focused on acceptance, curiosity, sincerity, and mindful speaking when she says, "Heather, I've seen you struggle with this for so long now, and it's paining me to see how hard this is on you. But I also see there's no real change in the situation. What keeps you from getting yourself out of this?"

Heather feels a little defensive. She hesitates and checks in with herself: What is really going on here? She knows Jada is on her side, and she knows she is right. Instead of responding out of defensiveness, she decides to unveil her fears of being a single mom, the financial issues she'll run into, and the struggle with her deep-seated beliefs about the need for children to grow up in a two-parent environment. She and Jada talk about each of them, and together they find a way forward that feels good to Heather. She decides to have the difficult conversation with her husband that has been coming for so long.

When the Relationship Is Unbalanced

Some friends have the habit of taking more than they give. They may take time, attention, and money (expecting others to pay for them), or they may talk more than they listen.

When this happens once or twice, it is probably just part of the ebb and flow of a longer friendship where trust is already established. It's not necessary to have an exactly equal amount of giving versus taking, and it's unwise to keep track of it. But in some cases it becomes blatantly obvious that balance is lacking. How do you bring that up?

However awkward it may feel, it is important to be clear about what you need, even when it feels a little vulnerable to start the conversation.

Be prepared to listen to what your friend says in return. You may feel it's important to call her every few days to chat, but she may think this is a little much and would rather meet in person every two weeks or so.

You could say something like this to open the conversation: "I'm happy to listen to everything you're going through, and I would also like to be able to share my experiences with you. Could you listen to what's going on with me?" or "Yes, I can pay for lunch, and since I have paid for our lunches the last couple of times, I will send you a reminder to pay me back."

Mindful Attitudes to Bring In Regarding a Friendship Imbalance

- Self-disclosure
- Sincerity
- Mindful speaking
- Mindful listening

When You Want to Deepen the Relationship

Mindful attitudes like tapping into the undercurrent and interconnection can be powerful tools to connect with your friends on a deeper level. To get there, you will sometimes have to bring up the fact that your friendship isn't as deep as it could be. Maybe you and your friend got stuck talking about the daily stuff, or maybe you sense your friend finds it a little scary to disclose more about themselves and be vulnerable. How can you bring this up without alienating them from you?

However noble and beautiful your goal is, you will have to treat this like you're offering your friend constructive feedback. You are saying something about how you two are together, which may indirectly be felt as an "attack" on your friend. As you've seen in Chapter 5, feedback is often met with hostility and defensiveness. To bring up this topic, you could use this format for giving feedback:

1. Say something genuinely positive about your friend. For example, say, "I love having you as my friend. You are always there for me when I need someone to talk to."

2. Say what you would like to do differently, from the perspective of your needs and feelings: "I've noticed, however, that I sometimes hold back my deepest feelings even from you, and that's a pity. I would like for us to be okay with being more open with each other."

3. Check if they understand so far, and if necessary explain a little further: "For example, when I told you about my problems at work, I did say it was painful how my boss responds to my work, but I didn't disclose how unappreciated and undervalued I felt, personally."

4. Listen to their response, and be open to hearing more than what they literally say. In this case, it's very simple for them to agree to what you're saying, and then, when push comes to shove, still not be open to sharing the deeper stuff. This will be clear from the way they respond to you: embracing the idea or keeping it a little vague.

5. Hear if there's more explanation needed. If you feel they do need that, say something to respond to where you feel the doubts are or the clarity is needed.

Mindful Attitudes to Bring In Regarding Deeping the Friendship

- Tapping into the undercurrent
- Self-disclosure
- Sincerity
- Mindful listening

When Friends Take Advantage of You

You may have some people around who call you only when they need help yet happen to always be unavailable when you need assistance. Because you value being there for your friends, and maybe because you find it hard to say no, people can always count on you. But what if it doesn't feel okay anymore?

This is an interesting challenge; it is as much about you as it is about them. Of course, it's important to be there for your friends and as long as it honestly feels okay to you, even when people do not offer you similar kindness in return, it's absolutely fine. However, if there's room for people to cross your boundaries, it's because you give them that space.

As soon as you start feeling that people are taking advantage of you, and you continue to engage with them, you put yourself in the drama triangle: either as the savior ("How would he be able to deal with this without my help?") or as the victim ("He is out to take advantage of me, and I cannot stop it").

The most straightforward way to handle this is to simply start setting better boundaries for yourself and do only the things that you want to do without expecting anything in return (not appreciation, love, a return favor—nothing).

To practice setting boundaries, follow these steps when someone asks you for a favor:

1. Keep yourself from saying "yes" right away—instead, pause.

2. Check in with yourself to feel inside: Is this a "yes" (without strings attached) or a "no"?

3. If it's a no, calmly state that you cannot help them. If it's really hard for you to say no, start small. You may want to try responses like "I am sorry, but I don't have time for that right now" or "I must prioritize [say what needs prioritizing] now." Or if you want be firm (and dive into a conversation about this), you could say, "I feel I have been doing you so many favors lately that I think you should ask someone else."

The reason you don't necessarily need to have a specific conversation about this is because the trouble started because you didn't protect your own boundaries. People are allowed to ask, and you can't expect them to read your mind. Open communication is a valuable thing in friendships. As soon as you stop saying "yes" when you want to say "no," the feeling that people take advantage of you will be gone.

To make it easier on yourself, tell some of your friends that you're practicing saying no sometimes because you have been saying yes to everything. They can help you stay on track and will understand what you're up to when you suddenly start saying no to their requests. An added advantage is that there will probably be at least a few who take this as a hint to not ask as much anymore.

Mindful Attitudes to Bring In Regarding Friends Taking Advantage of You

- Presence
- Sincerity
- Checking in with yourself

When You Feel Left Out

What happens when you find out that some of your friends have gone out together without inviting you? This may bring back some painful memories of another time you were left out. Or maybe you are able to rationalize your hurt away by thinking of a solid, rational reason why they excluded you. But if you're completely honest, you probably feel hurt and sad about it.

If you don't discuss this, it will probably be a lingering hurt in the back of your mind, which won't do your friendship any good. It may even make it harder to trust your friends after this. So if you value the friendship, it's important to have an open conversation about why they decided to go without you and if there is any effect on your relationship. How can you bring this up and explore what happened?

First, specifically work on bringing in an open mind and not jumping to any conclusions (nonjudgment). This doesn't mean you shouldn't honor your own feelings about what happened, though. It's important to share your side, even when it puts you in a vulnerable position. Your mindset is one of courage to bring it up and curiosity while listening. This is a great time to practice mindful speaking, and especially to stay away from the six pitfalls you learned in Chapter 6.

You could use a sentence like this to start the conversation: "I've found out that some of you went to/did [state the place or activity] without inviting me. I know that it's your right to choose whom to spend time with, so I'm not blaming you, but it did hurt my feelings, as I thought we were good friends. What happened?"

While listening to the explanation, stay completely present. Even if the message isn't a happy one, stop yourself from checking out. Stay connected to your body and be aware of your internal responses to what is being said. Handle it like you would handle constructive criticism: Open yourself up and listen to really understand what they say before asking clarifying and future-oriented questions (see the section in Chapter 5 called How to Listen to Constructive Criticism).

Mindful Attitudes to Bring In Regarding Being Left Out

- Open mind
- Nonjudgment
- Curiosity
- Mindful speaking
- Presence

CHAPTER SUMMARY

The following are takeaways, action steps, and reminders to support you in having those challenging talks with your friends and creating clarity and a deeper connection.

● Difficult situations with friends can be challenging because friendships are very important to us but can also be a little noncommittal as well. As there are no official binds between friends, it's potentially easier to let things slide. But like all relationships, friendships need maintenance to stay up to date, especially when life's circumstances change.

● The PAUSE approach supports you in challenges with your friends by reminding you to see them as they are right here, right now. Accept the challenge and take it on right away so it won't get out of hand, and embrace mindful speaking and the golden partnership of curiosity and sincerity.

● The fact that you (hopefully) feel safe with and appreciated by your friends makes it easier to tap into the undercurrent and disclose more about yourself. The appreciation and love you feel for your friends will probably allow you to stay in a mindful mindset and be open to synchronous events and ideas.

● Remember that in every challenging situation with a friend, you are still the co-owner of how the situation will unfold. The way you engage in the conversation has a huge impact on how things will go down, and finger pointing won't get you anywhere.

CHAPTER II
USING THE PAUSE APPROACH WITH COWORKERS

"Engage your emotions at work. Your instincts and emotions are there to help you."

Richard Branson

Do you always show your true self at work? Probably not—many people aren't able to show who they truly are and share what they really believe in their workplace. On the other hand, having a separate "professional persona" in addition to your real self makes it very complicated to work through any difficult situations using a mindful approach to conflict resolution. In this chapter, you will learn how to resolve difficult situations in the workplace and how you can deal with your feelings and potential vulnerability there. You will also discover how hierarchy, office politics, your professional persona, and the fact that you get paid influence difficult conversations at work. This chapter will also present a step-by-step model for having what we call "bad news conversations," in which the message you have to convey actually is the real issue. But first, let's look at what makes difficult conversations at work different from our private ones.

The Challenges of Difficult Conversations at Work

Difficult conversations at work are different from their private counterparts. On one hand, at work you generally feel a little less emotionally invested in the relationships you have. Even though colleagues may be important, generally they won't be at the same level as your friends and family.

On the other hand, work is often a highly important part of your life. That's not really surprising, given the eight or more hours you spend at your job daily and the fact that many people identify with their work quite intensely. People like to take pride in the work that they do and, ideally, that work shows the world something positive about them. Let's look closer at the elements that make the challenging situations at work specifically hard before setting out to learn how to navigate these in a mindful manner.

Your Professional Persona

Even if it doesn't seem like it, you are part of a social network at work that has its own social code and standards. Ideally, your personality fits your work environment like a glove. But more likely, it won't. And in those cases, there will be a (subconscious) call to adapt and conform to fit unwritten rules and standards. This can easily lead to adapting your personality to fit into a group that you didn't select because of that code, creating what is called a "professional persona."

Depending on the situation at work, this professional persona is a lot like the "regular" you but is a bit better suited to fit into the social group and cultural norms at work. Your professional persona will probably be more polished than your normal self. It may also be less funny, quirky, and outspoken. At some types of workplaces, your work persona might even be drastically different, like if you keep your romantic life or certain hobbies a secret.

Our Beliefs about Professionalism

Your professional persona is connected to everything in your iceberg that has to do with professionalism, effectiveness, and success. You don't have to be consciously aware of these beliefs for them to be influencing you from behind the scenes. These (sub)conscious beliefs about how to work and how to be at work are not always in line with your other conscious and subconscious ideas. For example, you can believe on one level that it is important for you to speak your truth but at the same time believe that it is not professional to contradict your manager in public.

This complicated dynamic can lead to being less open about your true motives and beliefs, and your colleagues will probably do the same. These hidden motives create interaction where you and your colleagues are trying to solve a problem on the wrong level of the conversation. Instead of tapping into the undercurrent to find the actual reasons for the dispute, you may stay at the upper level to try to solve your disagreements "objectively."

It's All about Content, or Is It?

Difficult situations at work most often start out as content-related, meaning that things between you and your colleagues get complicated because you have a disagreement on how to handle something you are hired to do (for example, which creative approach to take for a specific account in a PR firm, how to deal with a problematic child in a classroom, or even what medicine to prescribe for a specific patient). However, whenever people interact with people, icebergs are always a factor. When conversations become difficult, you can trust that there's always more going on than rational facts. But in a work environment, it's not that easy to bring out the feelings, motives, and values that play a role in the undercurrent.

When you do not express what you really experience because you want to keep things professional, these motives, beliefs, and feelings start having their own sideshow. They leak or even burst into the conversation, preventing you from really listening and being present, and affect your self-esteem and relationships.

Mindful Lesson: Sharing Needs

Leonard is an employee at a large corporation. He loves his job. Currently, he's working on a project that he feels quite passionate about. One day his manager, Ella, asks him about the progress he's made. As he explains what he's been working on, it's clear from the frustrated and impatient look on Ella's face that she's not enthusiastic about his approach. She gives him very detailed instructions on how to continue the project, which he feels won't lead to better results than his own approach. Leonard is really disappointed. He doesn't understand why Ella is taking control from him, and he's disappointed about her micromanaging the situation and her lack of appreciation for his chosen approach to this challenging project, but he nods and leaves the room.

Instead of voicing his disappointment and confusion, feelings that arise from somewhere deep in his iceberg, Leonard chooses the "professional approach" by accepting the feedback and getting back to work. Feeling insecure and underappreciated, he now has to work with the instructions his manager gave him. In no time he begins to feel disconnected from the project and his sense of ownership is diminished, but he continues to try to make the most of it, in alignment with his beliefs about professional behavior.

Ella doesn't know about Leonard's disappointment, confusion, and insecurity, or the lack of appreciation he feels. However, she senses that Leonard is not really motivated, which is not like him at all. She wonders what to make of that: Maybe he isn't into big projects like this? Or maybe he's not equipped to handle them? She decides to have another talk with him. She tells him she sees he is less motivated and asks him why. Leonard decides to take this chance to be open, and he discloses his frustration about their previous talk. He says, "I would have been glad to discuss your ideas, of course, but you just took over without any discussion, which was quite demotivating. It made me feel underappreciated and insecure."

Ella is glad she opened the conversation: "Thank you for sharing this with me, Leonard. I know it isn't easy to be open about these things. And I am sorry I was brisk earlier. I had had a rough couple of meetings before I met up with you, and I projected that onto our meeting. I didn't take the time to sit with you and really listen and discuss."

Leonard and Ella agree that next time, Leonard will be more open about what he needs from Ella. They also come up with a way to handle the project that includes the most important elements from both of their approaches.

The Hierarchy Issue

Even though more and more companies try to be flatter and less hierarchical, in most work environments your relationships and interactions will be influenced by position. Related to hierarchy is the topic of office politics—something you may be trying to avoid at all costs. Unfortunately, unless you work at an organization that is deeply invested in creating a politics-free culture, you will probably have to work with it. Performance is most often not the only way you are being evaluated, which makes it fair to say that being at least a bit politically savvy seems to be a smart way to move ahead in your company. (Of course, being politically savvy doesn't mean you have to stoop to the lower levels of office politics, like backstabbing, gossiping, shooting people down, and not really working together with others.)

In handling difficult situations related to hierarchy or office politics, it's essential to understand that even though someone may be higher or lower in rank, your value and equality as people are nonnegotiable, and you are always the co-owner of the situation.

The Payment Issue

The fact that your livelihood depends on you staying employed—and you staying employed depends on what people think about your performance—complicates the questions of whether and when to bring up disagreements and conflicts. Aspects of the mindful approach, such as openness to experience, nonjudgment, and nonattachment, are more complicated when this kind of dependence is part of the equation.

The exchange of money for time, effort, and thinking power can create a sense of obligation to comply with the organization. You may feel that, because they pay you, you have no real right to disagree or challenge. On the other hand, being paid for something can also inspire you to not let matters bottle up as you may otherwise be tempted to do. Plus, when difficult situations arise, you may feel called to resolve them, as you see this as part of your job.

It's helpful to keep reminding yourself that getting paid doesn't mean you are being bought. In weighing up the pros and cons of starting a difficult conversation, you may want to consider what approach will lead to the most self-respect. What will allow you to look at yourself in the mirror and fully embrace how you handled the situation?

How the Mindful Approach Will Support You

At work, the biggest challenge is to approach the problems you face as the person you are, and not as a "worker bee." So even though it may take courage to be open about what is going on for you, it will help steer the conversation to the issues that really matter. The PAUSE approach will be truly helpful.

Presence

At work, you may easily find yourself being in your head all the time. To feel what you are really experiencing in the moment, you will need to activate the connection to your body. You can help yourself become fully present by taking a few deep breaths (you can do this anytime, without anyone noticing), which instantly creates a connection to your body, allowing you to sense the undercurrent and activate your intuitive mind.

Acceptance

Even though things at work may not be exactly as you would want them to be, acceptance helps you to focus on bringing positive change to the things within your circle of influence and leave the rest. It's not up to you to exchange the current CEO for someone who may do a better job, and your continuing focus on how bad the current one is doing her job will only drain your energy. Of course, that doesn't mean you just have to sit by and take it. If you feel her impact is making the people in the company suffer or the focus drift away from the company's reason for being, for example, it may be time to find a new position in a company where the CEO's tasks are done in a way you think is better.

Undercurrent

The case of Leonard and Ella earlier in this chapter shows how simple conversations at work can easily get difficult pretty quickly. It's so "normal" to not speak your mind that sometimes you may almost forget that you could speak your mind. But when you don't, people form all sorts of ideas about what may be going on. Everything that you don't say finds a place in the undercurrent. Bringing some of that into the actual conversation makes things a lot more straightforward.

You don't have to bring up everything, of course—your childhood hurts will probably not be relevant in most work situations—but there is a lot that is relevant. For example, your beliefs about professional behavior, your need to be acknowledged and appreciated, your need for validation, your ideas about your own intelligence, and so on, might come up.

Synchronicity

By diving beneath the surface, you will start a deeper conversation, which will lead to better solutions. By disclosing what you are thinking, you will invite your coworkers to do the same. And when you know what your counterpart is thinking, it's easier to find a solution that works.

Of course, it's essential to bring in the right mindset of interconnection and a win-win mentality and to trust the process. Especially at work, keep in mind that what is really important will present itself during the conversation itself. You may be used to preparing yourself half to death for high-profile presentations or meetings, so remember to prepare, but not too well, and trust that the right words will be available to you when they are needed.

Exchange

Before responding from your official position or your preconceived idea of how things must be solved, take a pause. Asking yourself the powerful question of "What is really going on here?" works really well as an opening into the undercurrent. By asking this out loud, you introduce the opportunity for people to go a little deeper and disclose a few of their preoccupations.

Speaking sincerely is just as important at work as it is in your personal life. People who say what they really believe to be true are somewhat rare in the workplace, which makes it extra impactful when someone does it. So do it! It builds instant connection.

Some Specific Situations

Let's explore a couple of common work situations. For each of these, you'll find a suggestion on how to approach it and an overview of the mindful attitudes that will best serve you when taking on this topic at work.

When You Don't Agree with Your Manager

Let's circle back to the case study about Leonard and Ella for a minute. What would have happened if Leonard had dared to mention his true thoughts and feelings during that first conversation with his manager? Many people are scared off from this, but if you don't say something, the undercurrent will get to work, which results in assumptions and premature conclusions that may have horrible effects on careers. How can PAUSE support you here?

Of course, your manager is in charge and has the final say about the course things will take. Bringing in some acceptance to acknowledge that will be wise. Nonetheless, managers don't know everything, and you have probably spent a lot of time finding the right approach. Respecting that compels you to at least give some pushback.

Even if you were too taken aback by the abruptness or harshness with which your manager rebuked your approach to immediately respond, there is always the opportunity to circle back to the conversation. Sharing what you really believe is the best way forward will make sure the discussion revolves around the right things, if nothing else. This alone makes it worthwhile. When you need to talk about not agreeing with your boss, a strong personal presence will support you, as you learned in Chapter 4. Before entering a meeting that requires you to be courageous, prepare your energy to set yourself up for success.

You could use a sentence like this to start the conversation: "Could we circle back to our previous conversation? It had quite an impact on me, and I wanted to check if I understood you correctly."

Who knows—maybe you will convince them, or maybe the undercurrent will supply you with a new approach that is even better than what either of you came up with.

Mindful Attitudes to Bring In Regarding Disagreements with a Boss

- A powerful presence
- Disclosing information from the undercurrent
- Sincerity
- Empathy and interconnection

When You Need to Give Feedback to a Colleague

Sometimes it will be necessary to offer feedback to one of your colleagues. For example, maybe you're working on a project together and their contribution is late or not up to standards. Even though it may not be easy to do, it is part of a healthy workplace to be able to both give and receive constructive feedback. Please refer to the format for giving feedback to friends in Chapter 10 for guidance on how to do that.

When You Work with a Bully

You know you're working with a bully when one of your colleagues points out your mistakes, continues to bring them to your or even your boss's attention, gossips about you, tells lies to your coworkers, or sabotages your work. Being the victim of a bully is one of the most rotten situations to experience at work, and unfortunately it happens much more often than you might think. Just like dealing with a bully in high school, immediately running to your boss to solve it will probably not be the most effective solution, nor will it work well in this situation to have an honest conversation. Bullies need to be tackled by a powerful personal presence and a thoughtful, yet firm, policy. It's important to respond swiftly and directly to every attempt to belittle or hurt you.

So how do you go about this? First of all, focus on building up your personal presence when you interact with the bully. Go to the restroom before a meeting and strengthen your presence by practicing deep, centering breathing and setting your intention to show yourself respect and not allow yourself to be put down. Second, respond always and immediately by bringing the attention to their behavior: If the bully is gossiping behind your back, go to them and tell them that if they have a problem with X, they are very welcome to tell you directly. If they feel your skills at Y are not up to standards, inform them that your boss believes otherwise and you are not interested in their opinion.

By giving these kinds of cool, almost understated, responses to their behavior, you're putting them on notice. You don't need to be unfriendly or emotional—honestly, it's better not to. It is important, however, to keep up your game, as it will probably take at least two or three such responses to convey the message that you're not playing along. It may help you to inform a trusted colleague or friend about what's going on so they can support you.

If, after trying this approach for a while, they continue or start picking on someone else, do not avoid talking to your or the bully's manager. Behavior like that should really be banned from any workplace, and that need supersedes the mindful rule to not talk behind people's backs.

INSTEAD OF AFFIRMATIONS, USE QUESTIONS

Instead of using positive affirmations like "I can stop this bully" to change your negative self-talk, it turns out to be more helpful to formulate your goal in a question: "Will I be able to stop this bully?" The reason for this is that questions trigger your curiosity and problem-solving abilities instead of starting an internal war between your negative self-image and the positive statement.

Mindful Attitudes to Bring In When Handling a Bully

- A strong presence
- Deep breathing
- Positive intention
- Mindful speaking
- Trust in yourself

When You Have to Deliver Bad News

Bad news conversations are any conversations in which you have to say something you know for sure the other person does not like to hear, such as when you have to lay off or fire someone. The focus here is on bad news conversations related to people at work, but the structure you learn here is basically the same in personal situations (for example, if you want to break up with someone).

The late Rob Buckman, a University of Toronto professor of medicine, and Robert Bies, a Georgetown University professor of management, did years of research about how to deliver bad news in a successful manner. Bad news conversations tend to get emotionally charged very easily, but one positive from a communications standpoint is that they are quite straightforward content-wise. As long as you say what you need to say in a sincere and clear way, there is not that much that can go wrong.

Different from most conversations discussed in this book, bad news conversations are usually somewhat scripted. If you are the bringer of bad news, you will likely take specific steps to convey your message in a way that works for the company (including any legal requirements). The following steps are based on the work of Buckman focusing on delivering bad news to patients and Bies delivering bad news to employees, combining their best tips.

Step 1: Prepare, but Do Not Overprepare

You've heard it before: Preparation is good, but do not overdo it, even when you have to be the bringer of bad news. Even though the content and the facts are certainly relevant here, rehearsing your words until you memorize them is definitely a step too far. Here is what you should do to prepare.

- **Do not surprise:** If you have to let someone go because of poor performance, the bad news conversation in itself should not come as a surprise. Earlier performance interviews should have prepared your team member for this, because you have been clear about your expectations and have helped them in trying to step up their game.

- **Get the facts straight:** Write down or think about the main reasons why you've come to your decision. Consider how to phrase these in a factual way, staying away from opinion or judgment (so, say, "There are still too many inaccuracies in your work, like X, Y, and Z," instead of saying "Your work is sloppy").

- **Check the legal aspects:** Check with your HR or legal department to be sure you're in the clear regarding any relevant legal rights, regulations, and the things you are thinking of offering them.

- **Do not delay:** It is critically important to have the conversation as soon as is humanly possible. Things almost never suddenly become better. If there's an issue, it is always better to bring it up as soon as you notice, before things get worse or your response gets overheated because of the impact the mistakes have had. Bies says that "bad news delayed is bad news compounded." Especially when the impact of the conversation will be significant (for example, when laying someone off), having the conversation as soon as possible is the humane and respectful thing to do.

- **Consider the future:** In preparing, it's also helpful to think about ways you can support the other person after you've had the talk.

This way, when you ask them how you can help, you can offer a few tangible suggestions.

Step 2: Set the Stage

Make sure you are not busy when the other person comes in (for example, don't quickly finish up little things you could have done earlier, like going for coffee or sending a quick message to the babysitter). This requires you to plan the conversation in such a way that you have enough time in advance to wrap up everything that was going on before and to do some breathing exercises or take a short meditation break so you can indeed send out a calm and open energy.

Then, be mindful about creating a calm and open atmosphere for your discussion. Simply ask how they are doing and let them share a few things about their state of being, without asking for more details, before you take up your responsibility of saying what you need to say. Introduce it by saying something like "I am afraid I have some bad news..." or "This may not be what you want to hear, but...," without adding a meaningful pause afterward (so you don't drag it out).

Step 3: Break the News

After setting the stage, you should share the news in a straightforward and factual manner, using a short statement (about forty words should be enough). It's not necessary to go into the details right away; you can explain the situation further if needed after they have had a chance to respond.

OWN YOUR RESPONSIBILITIES

Do not ever use the technique of asking questions that invite the other person to basically "dig their own grave" ("How do you feel your performance has been the last few months?" for example). While it may free you from having to say what you are afraid of saying, it is unkind, rude, and basically running away from a task that really is yours to complete.

It's important to stay away from using humor metaphors, or any other technique to cloak your message, to avoid misunderstandings. There are examples of people who have been laid off but afterward weren't sure about the actual intention of the conversation.

Step 4: Handle the Emotions

Be prepared to handle emotions, because they almost certainly will arise. Bad news always brings out emotions, although depending on the situation and the person involved, the actual emotions may vary. People can respond with (shocked) silence, disbelief, anger, sadness, and more. It is your role to be the steadying factor and refrain from getting emotional yourself. At this stage, there is no need to explain your position further or ask for understanding. Accept whatever is happening and allow the other person to experience what is there for them. If there's a silence, allow for that. Only interrupt the silence with a gentle question you feel is appropriate, or by stating the emotion that is present: "I understand that you are upset/angry/sad" (see Chapter 4 for more detailed guidance on handling emotions).

Step 5: Explain Further

Once the emotions have settled down and the other person turns to you for clarification, they will often ask you for an explanation. If they aren't clear about whether they want to hear more, make sure you check before you start speaking. Be ready for sudden changes in emotional state (for example, they first express sadness; then ask, "But why?"; and immediately switch to anger as you start explaining).

When they are ready to hear a further explanation, give two or three reasons why you have made the decision. Phrase them in a factual but respectful way, and if you are asked to explain a specific point further, try to use some of the same words to avoid misunderstanding. Do not hold back any information for a later time. The time is now, and sharing what you know creates trust and openness.

Step 6: Help Find a Way Forward

After the message is clear, you can move to sharing the follow-up steps and offering concrete support, if appropriate. Follow-up steps are often related to the official procedure and can be pretty detailed. Sometimes it's better to share the overview and give them a handout with the detailed explanation to read at a later time, because you've just given them a lot to deal with. Offering support may feel nice to you, but it is not always appropriate. If the other person is still angry with you, it's hardly helpful to offer to drive them home. You may, however, ask if they need a moment alone before they collect their personal items.

Step 7: Wrap Up and Follow Up

When wrapping up the conversation, discuss what they will do next, and tell them who will inform colleagues about what has happened and when. After the conversation, follow up after a few days if your HR or legal department approves.

If you follow these steps, you can be confident that your conversation will be as good as it can be. Bad news conversations lead only to conflict if the other person feels they are badly handled (the process isn't executed well enough) or that they are not being heard. This of course doesn't mean that the receiver of the news agrees with the decision itself or refrains from following the normal legal procedure.

Mindful Attitudes to Bring In Regarding Delivering Bad News

- Being fully present
- Interconnection
- Mindful speaking
- Handling emotions

CHAPTER SUMMARY

The following are takeaways, action steps, and reminders to support you in having the conversations that matter at work.

● The primary issue is that difficult conversations at work are expected to be, well, about work. But other things creep in, too, because people are so personally invested in their jobs. Because being touched on a personal level and showing emotions at work are exactly what most people try to avoid at all costs, people tend to avoid discussing the underlying issues that created the work conflicts in the first place, which leads to superficial solutions, allowing the issues to fester and potentially pop up in other situations too. It requires added awareness and determination to navigate work-related challenges in a mindful way.

● The PAUSE approach will support you by helping you access the undercurrent and explore what is really going on. One of the most powerful and also simplest interventions is to (genuinely!) say, "I am wondering what this is really about." This invites people to add their two cents, which is almost always about something that is happening in the undercurrent.

● Bringing bad news is never easy, but it is possible to do it without being inhumane or unkind. The method offered here is a proven approach that combines thoughtfulness and clarity, and by offering room for emotions and time to let the message sink in, it will help the person receiving the bad news to accept the situation.

BIBLIOGRAPHY

Altman, Irwin, and Dalmas A. Taylor. *Social Penetration: The Development of Interpersonal Relationships.* New York: Holt, Rinehart and Winston, 1973.

Bies, Robert J. "The Delivery of Bad News in Organizations: A Framework for Analysis." *Journal of Management* 39, no. 1 (January 2013): 136–162. https://doi.org/10.1177/0149206312461053.

Bishop, Scott R., Mark Lau, Shauna Shapiro, Linda Carlson, Nicole D. Anderson, James Carmody, Zindel V. Segal, Susan Abbey, Michael Speca, Drew Velting, and Gerald Devins. "Mindfulness: A Proposed Operational Definition." *Clinical Psychology: Science and Practice* 11, no. 3 (September 2004): 230–241. https://doi.org/10.1093/clipsy.bph077.

Brown, Brené. *Daring Greatly: How the Courage to Be Vulnerable Transforms the Way We Live, Love, Parent, and Lead.* New York: Avery, 2012, p. 198.

Buckman, Robert. *How to Break Bad News: A Guide for Health Care Professionals.* Toronto: University of Toronto Press, 1992.

Burgo, Joseph. "The Health Benefits of Friendship." *Fix* (blog). March 9, 2015. www.fix.com/blog/health-benefits-of-friendship.

Chapman, Gary. *The Five Love Languages: How to Express Heartfelt Commitment to Your Mate.* Chicago: Northfield Publishing, 1992.

Emerald, David. *The Power of TED* (*The Empowerment Dynamic).* Bainbridge Island, WA: Polaris Publishing Group, 2005.

Friesen, Charity A. "What Pushes Your Buttons? How Knowledge about If-Then Personality Profiles Can Benefit Relationships." Thesis, Wilfrid Laurier University, 2010. www.researchgate.net/publication/241841463_What_Pushes_Your_Buttons_How_Knowledge_about_If-Then_Personality_Profiles_Can_Benefit_Relationships.

Kabat-Zinn, Jon. *Full Catastrophe Living: Using the Wisdom of Your Body and Mind to Face Stress, Pain, and Illness*, revised and updated edition. New York: Bantam Books, 2013.

Karpman, Stephen. "Fairy Tales and Script Drama Analysis." *Transactional Analysis Bulletin* 7, no. 26 (1968): 39–43. www.karpmandramatriangle.com/pdf/DramaTriangle.pdf.

Kraus, Michael W. "Voice-Only Communication Enhances Empathic Accuracy." *American Psychologist* 72, no. 7 (October 2017): 644–654. https://psycnet.apa.org/doiLanding?doi=10.1037%2Famp0000147.

McClelland, David C. *Human Motivation.* Cambridge: Press Syndicate of the University of Cambridge, 1987.

Ofman, Daniel. *Core Qualities: A Gateway to Human Resources.* Schiedam, Netherlands: Scriptum, 2001.

Rosenberg, Marshall B. *Nonviolent Communication: A Language of Life.* Encinitas, CA: PuddleDancer Press, 2015.

Senay, Ibrahim, Dolores Albarracín, and Kenji Noguchi. (2010). "Motivating Goal-Directed Behavior Through Introspective Self-Talk: The Role of the Interrogative Form of Simple Future Tense." *Psychological Science* 21, no. 4 (April 1, 2010): 499–504. https://doi.org/10.1177/0956797610364751.

Stone, Douglas, Bruce Patton, and Sheila Heen. *Difficult Conversations: How to Discuss What Matters Most.* London: Viking Penguin, 1999.

RESOURCES

Books

Bernstein, Gabrielle. *Judgment Detox: Release the Beliefs That Hold You Back from Living a Better Life*. New York: Gallery Books, 2018.

Brown, Brené. *Daring Greatly: How the Courage to Be Vulnerable Transforms the Way We Live, Love, Parent, and Lead*. New York: Avery, 2012.

Brown, Brené. *The Gifts of Imperfection: Let Go of Who You Think You're Supposed to Be and Embrace Who You Are*. Center City, MN: Hazelden, 2010.

Carson, Rick. *Taming Your Gremlin: A Surprisingly Simple Method for Getting Out of Your Own Way*. New York: HarperCollins, 2003.

Cuddy, Amy. *Presence: Bringing Your Boldest Self to Your Biggest Challenges*. New York: Little Brown and Company, 2015.

Faber, Adele, and Elaine Mazlish. *How to Talk So Kids Will Listen & Listen So Kids Will Talk*. New York: Scribner, 2012.

Kabat-Zinn, Jon. *Wherever You Go, There You Are: Mindfulness Meditation in Everyday Life*. London: Hyperion, 1994.

Lencioni, Patrick. *The Five Dysfunctions of a Team: A Leadership Fable*. San Francisco: Jossey-Bass, 2002.

Richo, David. *How to Be an Adult in Relationships: The Five Keys to Mindful Loving*. Boston: Shambhala, 2002.

Rosenberg, Marshall B. *Nonviolent Communication: A Language of Life*. Encinitas, CA: PuddleDancer Press, 2015.

Stone, Douglas, Bruce Patton, and Sheila Heen. *Difficult Conversations: How to Discuss What Matters Most*. London: Viking Penguin, 1999.

Tolle, Eckhart. *The Power of Now: A Guide to Spiritual Enlightenment*. London: Hodder & Mobius, 2005.

Tsabary, Shefali. *The Awakened Family: How to Raise Empowered, Resilient, and Conscious Children*. New York: Viking Penguin, 2016.

Online Resources

http://rosaliepuiman.com/mindfulconflictresolution
All the following online resources can also be reached through this site.

www.mindful.org/meditation/mindfulness-getting-started
This site offers a ton of information on mindfulness in general and the science behind mindfulness. It also offers several guided mindfulness meditations.

https://insighttimer.com
The InsightTimer App is a great resource for thousands of free guided meditations, including metta and mindfulness meditations.

http://rosaliepuiman.com/jumpstart
The "Self-Elevation Jumpstart" is a great way to start exploring your own iceberg and working on some of your (limiting) beliefs. The program is free and includes guided meditations by Rosalie Puiman.

www.youtube.com/watch?v=kgTL5G1ibIo&feature=youtu.be
Whitney Zweeres, PTA, teaches the diaphragmatic breathing technique.

https://transformationalpresence.org/store/audios/breathing-into-the-moment
"Becoming Mindful—Breathing Into the Moment," a guided exercise with Alan Seale.

www.youtube.com/watch?v=4Lb5L-VEm34
"Breathe to Heal," a TED Talk on how to use your breathing to heal anxiety and stress, by Max Strom.

www.youtube.com/watch?v=lt9OcLynjwE
Mingyur Rinpoche, a Tibetan Buddhist meditation master, explains the monkey mind.

www.youtube.com/watch?v=E_XSeUYa0-8&feature=youtu.be
Lauren Kress explains Karpman's drama triangle in five minutes.

**www.ted.com/talks/brene_brown_on_vulnerability?utm_
campaign=tedspread&utm_medium=referral&utm_source=tedcomshare**

"The Power of Vulnerability," a TED Talk, by Brené Brown.

www.youtube.com/watch?v=2n7FOBFMvXg&feature=youtu.be

Jon Kabat-Zinn explains the nine attitudes of mindfulness.

https://www.5lovelanguages.com

Website dedicated to the five love languages, including a test to discover yours.

https://greatergood.berkeley.edu/video/item/what_is_mindfulness

Jon Kabat-Zinn speaks about mindfulness and meditation.

https://www.youtube.com/watch?v=G1zPcBDUsl0

Self-disclosure (social penetration theory) illustrated by Jenna Rosenberry.

https://motheringanddaughtering.com

A website created by Sil Reynolds and Eliza Reynolds, a mother-daughter team, for other mothers and preteen and teen daughters.

www.ahaparenting.com/ages-stages/teenagers/parent-teen-relationship

Laura Markham creates "aha" moments for parents of kids from babies through teens.

https://psychcentral.com/blog/why-positive-affirmations-dont-work

Article by Sophie Henshaw about a more successful alternative to positive affirmations, based on research.

https://youtu.be/0MCPLor4CvM

Simon Sinek explains how to talk truth to power.

www.fastcompany.com/40503371/7-situations-where-vulnerability-is-the-best-management-strategy

Article by Harvey Deutschendorf on the value of vulnerability as a management strategy.

https://hbr.org/2016/01/what-to-do-when-you-dont-feel-comfortable-being-yourself-at-work

Article by Dorie Clark on how to handle not feeling comfortable at work.

INDEX